# TRUCKS

## THE WORLD'S GREATEST TRUCKS

# TRUCKS

## THE WORLD'S GREATEST TRUCKS

INGRID PHANEUF AND JAMES MENZIES

This is a Parragon book
First published in 2006

Parragon
Queen Street House
4 Queen Street
Bath BA1 1HE, UK



ISBN 1-40547-204-9

Editorial and design by
Amber Books Ltd
Bradley's Close
74–77 White Lion Street
London N1 9PF
www.amberbooks.co.uk

Project Editor: Sarah Uttridge
Design: Zoe Mellors
Picture Research: Terry Forshaw



A copy of the CIP data for this book is available from the British Library.

Printed in China

# CONTENTS

# Introduction

Trucks are unlike cars – not just because they are larger and more powerful but because they exist for different reasons. While cars gained popularity soon after their introduction in the late nineteenth century as glamorous toys for the rich, trucks were of the masses and for the masses. They were ugly, noisy and smelly and the only justification for their existence would be that they made sense. Economic sense.

What do we think about trucks? Why do we have to have them? Most people in the developed world are familiar with cars since they own one but the very same people often regard trucks as a blight on society. Those lumbering 'juggernauts' that clog up the highways are a source of frustration. Life, in their view, would be so much better if there weren't any trucks. Whichever view one takes, modern society relies on trucks. It is no exaggeration to say that we could not sustain our way of life without them.

In the century or so since horseless carriages became a reality, trucks have served an increasingly important role in industry and commerce. When the first self-propelled load carriers were invented in the late nineteenth century they were greeted with a mixture of suspicion, fear and even derision. Those early experimental machines were so crude and inefficient that they were not taken seriously. Such contraptions, it was thought, would never rival the horse-drawn wagon.

If one event gave credibility to the potential of motor trucks it was World War I. The rapid movement of troops and munitions revolutionised the way the war was fought. The post-war glut of ex-army trucks kick-started a new era of civilian road haulage. With that came an ever-growing network of main roads. Ironically, roads that were needed for the long distance transport of goods required trucks to help build them.

Once it became practical to haul heavy loads over long distances, society benefited from a wider choice of products. Supplies of perishable foods such as meat, fish, milk and fruit could be distributed over wider areas. Other important commodities such as fuel – coal, wood and oil – could be transported

Above: *The Western Star LowMax epitomizes what many North American owner/operators look for in a truck – a long, square bonnet, spacious sleeper cab and plenty of chrome.*

Above: *Cugnot's development of the steam dray was funded by the French King Louis XV.*

from the suppliers to the customer quickly and efficiently. True, such movement of goods began with the arrival of inland waterways and railways some half a century earlier but road haulage had the added benefit of a rapid door-to-door service.

During the first two decades of the twentieth century truck manufacturers explored various modes of propulsion including steam, gasoline and electric power. Both steam and electric vehicles had shortcomings in that their unladen weight was higher, limiting the 'payload', while the distance they could cover was also limited. The internal combustion engine emerged as the most efficient means of propulsion. That efficiency improved further with the arrival of the diesel engine in the mid-1920s.

In the early days there were large numbers of 'back-yard' truck builders some of whom flourished while others fell by the wayside. Many of the survivors grew into vast concerns, absorbing smaller manufacturers on the way. Trucks became progressively more efficient and capable of carrying heavier loads. Specialised bodywork enabled a wider variety of products to be transported safely and efficiently.

With the increase in road transport came the need for tighter legislation to govern the size, weight and performance of trucks. Such legislation, combined with innovative engineering, shaped the modern truck as we know it. Modern demands for even greater performance and driver comfort, increased safety and reduced emissions, have seen that process of development continue. Depending on their country of origin, today's trucks carry up to 30 tonnes (30 tons) at speeds of 90 km/h (56 mph) – a far cry from the solid-tyred bone-shakers of World War I when five tonnes was considered a big load and 20 km/h (12mph) a good speed!

Love them or loath them, trucks serve a vital role in our lives. Without them our stores, bars and filling stations would be empty. Without them manufacturing industry would grind to a halt as supplies of raw materials dried up. Just about everything we eat, drink, wear and use in our daily lives comes to us by truck.

Below: *While most drivers were forced to sit out in the open air, the Volvo series 1 trucks could be fitted with a cab on demand. This was probably due to the cold climate in Sweden.*

CUGNOT

1769 **France**

# CUGNOT'S STEAM DRAY

Built by French army officer Nicholas Cugnot, the 'grandfather' of the modern truck, this steam-powered truck was intended to transport cannons for the French army.

Inset: *Nicholas Cugnot's steam dray could carry up to 5 tonnes (5 tons) at 3.3 kph (2 mph) but could only generate enough steam to travel about 640m (700yds) before stopping to build up more steam.*

Left: *With a heavy boiler mounted ahead of its single front wheel Cugnot's vehicle was inherently unstable and is said to have collided with a stone wall whilst being demonstrated. Consequently its driver was responsible for the first recorded traffic accident.*

The steam dray had three wheels with iron rims, two at the back and one in front. The steam power came from a boiler hooked up to a two-cylinder engine, both of which were mounted over the front wheel of the vehicle. It could travel at 4km/h (2.48mph), stopping every 10 to 15 minutes to build up enough steam pressure to get going again.

In 1771, Cugnot built a second vehicle for testing which was a tractor designed for a 4- to 5-tonne (4- to 5 ton) payload. Cugnot sought the approval of France's Minister of War at the time, the Marquis de Monteynard, for some secret tests to be staged at Versailles. Secrecy was necessary at this time due to the fact that Cugnot and some of his highly placed supporters at the court of Louis XV viewed the steam dray as something of a national military secret. Despite this, the tests were never conducted, as the Minister did not give his approval or even answer Cugnot's letters.

## First truck accident

Tests were conducted, nevertheless, and the vehicle was soon credited with causing the world's first truck accident by colliding with a garden wall. In spite of such accidents, one of Cugnot's vehicles survived the French Revolution and today resides in the National Academy of Arts and Sciences in France.

Cugnot and his steam-powered vehicles faded into obscurity immediately after the Revolution however, as Napoleon took little interest in steam-powered gun tractors.

## Specifications

**Country:** France
**Year manufactured from:** 1769
**Engine:** two cylinder, steam powered
**Transmission:** not available
**Payload:** 4 tonnes (4 tons)
**Applications:** cannon ball carrier
**Special features:** one powered wheel in front

TREVITHICK
1803 UK

# LONDON STEAM CARRIAGE

In 1803, Richard Trevithick and his associate Andrew Vivian designed the London steam Carriage, a coach-like, steam powered vehicle capable of going up to 16km/h (9.9mph).

Right: *Though built to carry passengers, Trevithick's London Steam Carriage could, in theory, have been adapted to carry up to half a ton of goods. However, it would have been rather top-heavy and, being a tricycle, none too stable.*

James Watt was the first to patent 'parallel motion' in steam engines, which could keep a rigid piston rod moving vertically while attached to the end of an oscillating beam. He was also one of the first to use a definite measurement to compare steam-power to horsepower: one horsepower was measured precisely as 33,000 foot-pounds of work per minute. Within a few years, Watt's engines were frequently referred to as 14-horse engines, 20-horse engines, and so on.

## The London Carriage

Following on from Watt's ideas, in 1803, Trevithick (who also worked with Watt) and his associate Andrew Vivian assembled the London Carriage at Felton's carriage works at Leather Lane. On completion, the carriage was driven about 16km (10 miles) through the streets of London with seven or eight passengers, in an attempt to demonstrate to the public that self-powered passenger and/or cargo vehicles were a possibility.

While the experiment was considered successful, the vehicle proved highly unpopular, mainly because it terrified horses, but also because of several deaths due to horrific boiler accidents. There was also the issue of fires caused by sparks from the funnels. The media and public largely ignored the London Carriage and the vehicle was eventually dismantled.

## Specifications

**Country:** UK
**Year manufactured from:** 1803
**Engine:** two cylinder, steam powered
**Transmission:** not available
**Payload:** not available
**Applications:** experimental
**Special features:** first self-powered passenger carrying vehicle in the world

BOLLÉE

🛠 **1873 France**

# L'OBÉISSANTE

Amédée Bollée was one of the most ingenious French engineers of his time. Despite its old-style design, L'Obéissante was a very advanced steam vehicle.

Left: *Frenchman Amédée Bollée did much to advance steam carriage design with his l'Obéissante which was the first vehicle to feature Ackerman-type steering controlled by a steering wheel.*

Amédée Bollée was born in 1844. His father was a bell founder in the city of Le Mans. At first, the young Amédée worked in the foundry shop, where he perfected a new casting process. In 1867, he visited the French Exposition Universelle in Paris. There he saw steam carriages, and as an engineer took interest in this vehicle and began to work on a new project. Three years after the 1870 Franco-Prussian war, the steam carriage L'Obéissante (the Obedient One) was ready. The vehicle contained real craftsmanship, with accommodation for 12 passengers, a roof and windows, the overall style being like that of a train passenger car. The quiet steam boiler at the rear was another masterpiece. It burned 50kg (110lb) of coal per hour and the two cylinders under the floor could move l'Obéissante from 15 to 40km/h (9 to 25mph). This amazing top speed (for the time) was offset by a small range of 25km (16 miles). But the most advanced design within the steam carriage was the steering wheel, the first one in the automotive industry.

## Disappointment

After trials, l'Obéissante proved itself a very capable vehicle, and at the end of 1875 it made Le Mans to Paris (183km/114 miles) in only 18 hours. Bollée, however, was unable to sell the vehicle.

## Specifications

**Country:** France
**Year manufactured from:** 1873
**Engine:** steam with two cylinders
**Transmission:** not available
**Payload:** up to 12 passengers
**Applications:** utility steel truck
**Special features:** first steering wheel, independent front suspension, full forward control

BENZ
🛠 **1885–89 Germany**

# BENZ MOTOR WAGEN

Unlike steam engines, the internal-combustion engine operates by burning fuel inside the engine. With the introduction of the four-stroke internal-combustion engine from 1885, the era of the true truck begins.

Right: *Carl Benz perfected the first practical internal combustion-engined vehicle – a three-wheeled 'motor wagen'. It was powered by a horizontal single-cylindered engine which could run on petrol, paraffin or naptha.*

## Specifications

**Country:** Germany
**Year manufactured from:** 1885
**Engine:** four stroke internal combustion powered by paraffin, petrol or naptha
**Transmission:** not available
**Payload:** not available
**Applications:** experimental
**Special features:** three wheels

The forerunner of trucks powered by internal-combustion engines was a Benz three-wheeler. It could run on paraffin, petrol or naphtha, and could reach 15km/h (9.3mph). Benz's first motorized vehicle eventually featured three innovations that are still in use in trucks and cars today – an electric battery, spark plug and electric coil ignition – but not immediately. Benz's first electric ignition used a generator, but the generators of the early 1880s were not up to the task, so the inventor shifted to a storage battery. The vehicle's spark plug consisted of two lengths of insulated platinum wire stuck into the combustion chamber.

### No fuel injection

The fuel induction system also left something to be desired. The engine didn't use fuel injection or anything resembling a true carburettor. Instead, fuel drained into a can filled with fabric fibres and then evaporation carried the fumes into the cylinder.

Even so, the vehicle's four-stroke engine worked, the four strokes of the engine consisting of intake, compression, power, and exhaust. And after a major reorganization of the company in 1890, the Benz motor works was on its way to becoming a successful manufacturer of vehicles.

PEUGEOT
**1895 France**

# PEUGEOT TYPE 13

The Peugeot brothers introduced five units of the Type 13, the company's first petrol-powered truck, in 1895. The truck was a light delivery van, with a Daimler internal-combustion engine.

## Specifications

**Country:** France
**Year manufactured from:** 1895
**Engine:** petrol powered internal combustion
**Transmission:** chain drive
**Payload:** 400kg (882lb)
**Applications:** light delivery van
**Special features:** first commercial vehicle by Peugeot

Left: *France's earliest light delivery truck was based on the Peugeot Type 13 of which five were produced as early as 1895. They were powered by Daimler petrol engines.*

In 1888, Armand Peugeot's fascination with motorized vehicles was born. He proudly unveiled a Peugeot steam-powered tricycle at the Paris World Fair. But he also started to experiment with petrol-powered engines, and produced four units of the first petrol-powered four-wheel car, called the Type 2, fitted with a Daimler engine at the Valentigney factory.

It would soon include solid rubber or optional Michelin tyres with rubber tubes, thanks to Edouard Michelin, who tried out his pneumatic tyres on the company's Éclair model car in the Paris–Bordeaux–Paris race of 1895.

### Heavy-duty production

By 1900 Peugeot was manufacturing several heavy-duty vehicles (for that time) including the Type 18 eight-seater bus with proprietary Peugeot engine (Armand stopped buying Daimler's engines from Panhard and Levassor in 1896), the Type 22 two-seater pickup truck and the Type 32 wagonette-tonneau (21 units in 1900). The Type 34 and 35 commercial vehicles quickly followed. The Type 36 single-cylinder was the first tonneau with a bonnet at the front and a steering wheel with an inclined steering column instead of handlebars. It marked Peugeot's move to chainless transmission.

W.J. STILL
1899 Canada

# W.J. STILL ELECTRIC DELIVERY WAGON

Less than a year after Robert Simpson purchased his Fischer No. 2 Coach Delivery Wagon, Parker Dye Works purchased a Toronto-made electric delivery wagon from the W. J. Still Motor Company.

## Specifications

**Country:** Canada

**Year manufactured from:** 1899

**Engine:** battery powered electric

**Transmission:** belt driven, rear wheel drive

**Payload:** not available

**Applications:** delivery

**Special features:** Ackerman type steering

Above: *Like all electric vehicles the Still was limited to local deliveries since its batteries needed regular re-charging. It did, however, boast some advanced features including Ackerman steering.*

The wagon surely provoked the envy of the Fischer wagon driver, as the driver of the Still wagon was provided with lower seating under a protective roof. The motor was mid-mounted, with a belt driving the rear wheels.

### Ackerman steering

The Still wagon was also more stable, thanks to the inclusion of Ackerman-type steering. The Ackerman Steering Principle defined the geometry that is applied to all vehicles (two or four wheel drive) to enable the correct turning angle of the steering wheels to be generated when negotiating a corner or a curve. Before the principle was developed, horse-drawn carriages had parallel steering arms and suffered from poor steering performance (tending to tip while cornering at high speeds especially). Rudolf Ackerman is credited with working out that using angled steering arms would cure these vehicles of such steering problems.

Electric cars and trucks enjoyed popularity both in North America and Europe at the turn of the century.

SAURER

1903 **Switzerland**

# SAURER FIVE-TONNER

The first Saurer truck was built by Adolph Saurer at his factory in Arbon, Switzerland, in 1903. It grossed 5.08 tonnes (5 tons), and was powered by a four-cylinder, T-head, 18.6 to 22.3kw (25 to 30hp) engine.

Above: *The 1903 Saurer 5-tonner was unusual for a heavy truck of that period in featuring shaft drive. However, soon after production commenced this was changed to chain drive.*

The truck proved popular, collecting trophies at several international contests. Factories were erected in Paris and Lindau, Germany, and the company started distributing in Russia, Canada and Japan. The trucks first appeared in the US in 1911. By then Saurer trucks ranged from 1.52 to 3.55 tonnes (1.5 to 3.5 tons), all of them with four-cylinder engines producing 11.9 to 22.3kw (16 to 30hp) and four-speed transmissions. The smaller trucks were shaft-driven, while the larger ones used chains.

The trucks were so successful in Europe that by 1914, Saurer was producing 130 different models. The company's success continued into World War I, when the company's Paris factory produced military trucks. (They were converted for use as postal trucks after the war.) Throughout that period, many Saurer trucks continued to use wooden wheels, even though the general industry trend was towards solid rubber. Engines came in 5.3-, 6.8- and 8.1-litre (321.7, 412.7 and 491.6ci) sizes, with outputs of 31.3, 38.7 and 46.2kw (42, 52 and 62hp).

## From solid to pneumatic tyres

By the end of the 1920s Saurer trucks had finally made the transition to solid rubber and then pneumatic tyres, and many trucks were using diesel. In diesel use, at any rate, Saurer was a leader. It would be 10 years before other truck manufacturers began to use diesel extensively.

The 1930s saw the birth of the C-line series, which ranged in weight from 1.016 to 6.09 tonnes (1 to 6 tons). Smaller models contained four-cylinder, 2.8-litre (169.9ci), 37.2kw (50hp) diesel engines, or six-cylinder, 2.9-litre (176ci), 38.7kw (52hp) petrol engines. When fuel supplies were scarce during World War II, the trucks came with wood-gas generators as well.

A product of World War II, and one of Saurer's most impressive achievements, was the heavy-duty M4H, used for transporting ammunition. The tractor was forward control (meaning the driver sat ahead of the front axle and by definition the engine) with four-wheel drive and a four-cylinder, 52.1kw (70hp) engine with a 1.52-tonne (1.5-ton) capacity. By the standards of the day, it was extremely powerful.

Below: *The 1930s saw the birth of the C-line series, which included one- to six-tonners.*

## Specifications

**Country:** Switzerland

**Year manufactured from:** 1903

**Engine:** four cylinder petrol powered

**Transmission:** shaft or chain driven, four-speed

**Payload:** up to 2.54 tonnes (2.5 tons)

**Applications:** delivery, military

**Special features:** T-head engine

AUTOCAR

🛠 **1908 USA**

# AUTOCAR XVII

The original Autocar company began as the Pittsburgh Motor Car Company, founded in 1897 by brothers Louis and John Clark. Two years later, they moved the company to Pennsylvania, and renamed it Autocar.

Above: *Early Autocar trucks were of 2.03 tonnes (2 tons) payload capacity and of forward control layout which the company claimed to provide more even weight distribution and greater load space within the overall length.*

The company began focusing on trucks in 1907, with the introduction of the Autocar Model XVII – a two-cylinder 2.03-tonne (2-ton) truck with shaft-driven axle. By 1911, the company had switched over to making trucks exclusively.

The Autocar truck chassis quickly earned the reputation of lending itself to almost every style of body, a foreshadowing of the truck's forthcoming use in multiple applications. In 1925, Autocar advertised in the *National Petroleum News* that 'More even weight distribution on all four wheels is an added Autocar advantage for hauling shifting loads of petrol and oil.' In 1926, the company introduced the Autocar Model 26, a four-cylinder 5.08-tonne (5-ton) vehicle. A six-cylinder, cab-forward design was introduced in 1930.

## First diesel engines

In 1935, the first diesel engines, supplied by Kenosha, were introduced. By 1940 Autocar offerings included heavy trucks with a variety of tractions, including 6x2s, 6x4s, 6x6s and even 8x4s.

Autocar was the first truck manufacturer to build wheels with wooden instead of wire spokes, and is credited by automotive historians with several other truck-making firsts. It was the first company to mass-produce a truck with forward control (a configuration in which more than half the engine length is behind the furthest-front point of the windscreen base and the steering wheel hub is in the first quarter of the vehicle length). It offered the first four-cylinder-engine forward-control truck. And it was one of the few truck manufacturers to make its own engines, transmissions and rear axles. In addition, some historians cite Autocar trucks as being instrumental in the Allied forces' victories in both World Wars.

## Advertisements appeal to patriotism

A print advertisement published in 1943 cashed in on the patriotic sentiment aroused by the Autocar at that time:

'TANKERS AWEIGH! Massive, six-wheel tank trucks . . . for the Navy . . . Bristling Half Tracks for the Army . . . Rugged mobility for the Marine Corps and the Air Forces . . . All essential. All for Uncle Sam. All training the men and women of Autocar to build the sturdy, dependable Autocar Truck that the world will need when war is won. So keep your pledge to the U. S. Truck Conservation Corps. Your trucks are your own, but their life belongs to the Nation.'

Autocar obtained US government authorization for heavy-duty hauling in 1945, a fact the company did not hesitate to boast of in print advertisements:

'HEAVY TANKAGE! For the ruts of War or the highway of Peace, Autocar Trucks are precision-built for the heaviest of heavy-duty work. Mile after mile, day after day, year after year, these famous trucks put on dependable, low-cost-per-mile performance and reduced hauling and delivery costs for the nation's leaders. Ask Shell Union Oil Corporation. They know Autocar Trucks through long years of rugged use... Follow the leaders, for they know the way,' reads an advertisement printed in 1945.

## White buys controlling interest

The White Motor Car Co. purchased a controlling interest in Autocar in 1953, and White was purchased by Volvo in 1981. In 1988, Volvo GM Heavy Truck Corp. was formed as a joint venture between Volvo and General Motors Corp. At the time, Volvo GM's nameplates were WHITE GMC and Autocar. The WHITE GMC nameplate was discontinued in 1995 and Volvo GM's trucks were sold under the Volvo and Autocar nameplates, the latter continuing to appear on heavy-duty construction trucks.

In July 2001, Grand Vehicle Works Holding Corporation (GVW) announced the purchase of the AutoCar Class 8 Xpeditor truck line from Volvo. Called LCF trucks (Low Cab Forward) the trucks were used primarily used in the vocational market. Autocar celebrated its 100th birthday in 1997.

## Specifications

**Country:** USA
**Year manufactured from:** 1908
**Engine:** two cylinder petrol powered
**Transmission:** three-speed
**Payload:** 2.03 tonnes (two tons)
**Applications:** multiple, body customized for buyer
**Special features:** Chassis lent itself to almost every style of body

Left: *After 1919 Autocar moved up the weight range with models capable of carrying 3.04 tonnes (3 tons), 4 tonnes (4 tons) and 5.08- tonne (5-ton) payloads. Forward control was the norm until 1926 when conventional trucks were added to the range.*

RENAULT
**1910 France**

# RENAULT TRUCK

The 1910 Renault was built for versatility. It was used for a variety of applications, including delivery vans and general urban transport. The Renault story started in 1898, when Louis Renault founded the company.

By 1900, production rose to 179 cars and by 1903, Renault had built its first heavy-duty (for the time) chassis for commercial use. The chassis earned the company a contract for supplying Paris taxis and was partially responsible for production climbing to 1200 units in 1905. In 1907, Renault had produced a bus, and introduced it in 10- and 15-seater versions at the Ninth Paris Motor Show.

As was the case with many early 1900s truck makers, Renault owed a great deal of its success as a heavy-duty chassis manufacturer to the war. By 1917, Renault was producing the 'Diamond brand' design – the first modern tank. The company produced 30 of these tanks per day at its plant in Vernisseaux.

## Award winners

By the mid-1920s, Renault tractors and 7.1-tonne (7-ton) trucks were garnering awards. The company was the first to offer a road tractor fitted with a Servo vacuum assisted brake. Renault also manufactured trucks powered by gas generators to promote the use of fuels other than petrol.

The scheme succeeded, as by the 1930s Renault was producing diesel-powered trucks. Unfortunately the Nazi occupation of France in WWII temporarily tarred the company's reputation – its trucks were extensively used by Germany.

After the war, Louis Renault was found guilty of collaboration and as a result, the company was confiscated and nationalized.

Above: *This 1909 model has a sloping bonnet which was a characteristic of all early Renaults.*

## Specifications

**Country:** France
**Year manufactured from:** 1910
**Engine:** petrol powered
**Transmission:** not available
**Payload:** not available
**Applications:** multiple, chassis also used for taxis
**Special features:** built for versatility

FEDERAL

1910 USA

# FEDERAL TRUCK

In its newsprint advertisements, the Federal Motor Truck Company of Detroit, Michigan, proclaimed itself the 'largest manufacturer of 4.57 and 3.55 tonne (4½ and 3½ ton) worm drive motor trucks exclusively.'

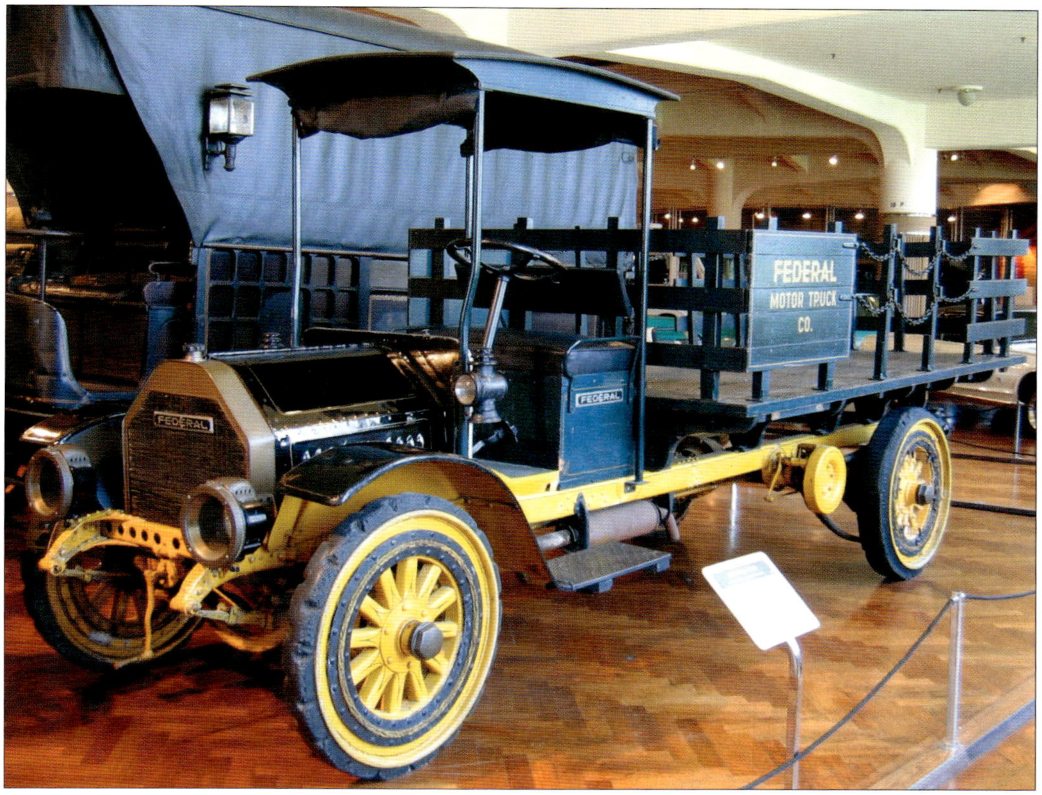


Right: *What originated as the Bailey Motor Truck Co became the Federal Motor Truck Co and the first chain drive 1-tonner of 1910 was based on a Bailey prototype. Power came from a 4-cylinder petrol engine.*

## Specifications

**Country:** USA
**Year manufactured from:** 1910
**Engine:** petrol powered
**Transmission:** belt drive
**Payload:** 1.016 tonne (one ton)
**Applications:** haulage, agricultural, delivery, municipal
**Special features:** by 1920s Federal trucks were being exported overseas

At that time, Federal mainly manufactured trucks that could carry a 1.016-tonne (1-ton) payload. The 1910 design was conventional, and looked much like a car, with its radiator and petrol engine in the front and its driver sitting behind it under a metal awning.

It had spoked steel wheels with solid rubber tyres, and the chassis had two frames rails which appear to be as close together as a car's. (The wheels however, were set out from the frame rails, making it easier for them to fit into the ruts that were typical of many American roads at that time.) The truck could reach speeds of up to 32km/h (20mph).

### Ford an early convert

Henry Ford, of the Ford Motor Company, would buy the very first model, fitted out with a wood slat box atop a flatbed, for use on his farm. This vehicle survives in the Henry Ford Museum in Dearborn Michigan to this day. Ford was one of the truck's earliest converts, as commercial motor vehicles were, at that time, still competing with horse-drawn carriages. Indeed, many motor truck advertisements of the time pointed out how motorized transport was a more cost-effective haulage method than horse-drawn carriages. Federal was not alone in trying to convince the potential truck buyers of this.

MACK

**1916 USA**

# MACK AC 'BULLDOG'

The Mack AC truck was introduced in 1916. With its chain-drive rear axle, the truck soon earned a reputation for reliability and durability. It saw continued success, remaining in production for 24 years.

Above: *The Mack AC 'Bulldog' had a formidable reputation for toughness. British soldiers in World War I were so impressed by its tenacity that they nicknamed it 'Bulldog'. Mack subsequently adopted the quintessentially British breed as its company emblem.*

Even before World War I, Mack had established a good international reputation. The company had already built many British military trucks, as well as an armoured car on an AB chassis for the New York National Guard.

Chief engineer Edward Hewitt was credited with designing Mack's AC model, which had 18 patents to cover all of its innovations. The truck's radiator was placed behind its engine, and air was drawn from the bonnet, forced through the radiator, and then sent through screening at the front. This unique design was believed to prevent damage to exposed radiators that was apparently being caused, accidentally or not, by anti-truck lobbyists. (At the time it was led by US trade unionists who feared, justifiably as it turns out, that motorized vehicles would put horse-drawn transport out of business.)

Another innovation was the positioning of the steering wheel at a 45 degree angle, which would prove to be considerably more comfortable for the driver. As for the engine, it was rated at 55.18kw (74bhp: the acronym for 'Brake Horsepower' referring to the actual or useful horsepower of an engine, usually determined from the force exerted on a friction brake or dynamometer connected to the drive shaft). The press chrome-nickel steel frame rails were heat-treated for durability, as were the pair-cast cylinders. Lightweight aluminium was used for the radiator tank, the transfer case, the timing cover and the engine crankcase. The front axle was made of dropforged alloy steel, however, to make the AC tougher.

### Selective transmission

The AC had a selective three-speed transmission and a clutch brake. It also had an all-steel cab with an optional metal roof; a substantial improvement on the more common exposed wooden seats of the day. The design proved extremely popular. During World War I, Mack delivered approximately 4500 AC model trucks of 3.55-tonne (3.5-ton), 5.58-tonne (5.5-ton), and 7.62-tonne (7.5-ton) capacity for the US government, which had adopted the truck as a standard military vehicle. These went overseas to France with American doughboys.

Mack also produced and delivered over 2000 units to Great Britain during the same period. British soldiers reportedly referred to Macks as 'bulldogs,' calling out 'Aye, send in the Mack Bulldogs!' when faced with a difficult transport problem. British engineers and soldiers apparently believed the trucks had the tenacity of a bulldog. As the bulldog was the symbol of Great Britain at that time, this was high praise indeed. The Americans needless to say, shared the opinion of the British, at least according to company historians. Of course, the nickname could also easily have been due to the appearance of the trucks, with their snub noses. Whatever the case, the nickname stuck. AC and Mack trucks in general would eventually became widely known as 'the Bulldog Macks,' and by 1922 the company adopted the Bulldog as its corporate symbol.

### Bulldog mascot

As for bulldog bonnet mascot, it wouldn't come along until much later. First, a picture of a bulldog (first drawn in 1921) would appear on a sheet metal plate riveted to each side of the cab, showing the bulldog chewing up a book entitled 'Hauling Costs', with the word 'Mack' on his collar and the words 'International Motor Company' underneath. (The name of the company, which had been changed to International Motor Company after a merger with two other truck makers, would be changed back to Mack in 1922 due to the fear the company would be confused with another US truck maker, the International Harvester Company.)

Left: *In frontal appearance the Mack AC, with its radiator behind engine layout, bore an uncanny resemblance to the French Renault. Ironically Mack was eventually absorbed into Renault Véhicules Industriels in 1990.*

Below: *Even before World War I, Mack had established an international reputation.*

## Specifications

**Country:** USA
**Year manufactured from:** 1916
**Engine:** petrol powered
**Transmission:** three-speed selective with clutch brake
**Payload:** 1.016 to 7.63 tonnes (one to seven and a half tons)
**Applications:** delivery, military
**Special features:** radiator behind engine

FORD TT
1917 USA

# FORD TT ONE-TONNER

Henry Ford built his first experimental commercial vehicle – a panel truck – in 1899. But it wasn't until 1917 that the Ford Motor Company brought out the TT one-tonner – basically a beefed-up Model T car.

A machinist's apprentice at the tender age of 16 in 1863, Ford's engineering skills had become evident from an early age. He soon became chief engineer for the Edison Illuminating Company in Detroit, Michigan. By 1903 Ford and a group of investors, who believed in his genius, had founded the Ford Motor Company.

## First Ford truck

The first commercial vehicle produced by the company was the Model E delivery wagon (a later version of the panel truck mentioned above). It proved useful for city deliveries and Ford Motors would continue to manufacture it through 1911. By then Ford had become known mainly for light truck and car manufacturing. Most famous of all, of course, was Ford's Model T car, otherwise known as the 'Tin Lizzy'.

But Henry Ford soon gained renown as an industrialist as well. Ford became the first automotive manufacturer (and the first North American manufacturer) to introduce

Above: *Henry Ford's legendary Model T was joined by a heavier model, the TT 1-tonner, in 1917. The simple rugged low-cost workhorse took the truck market by storm.*

assembly-line production to his factory. He was also the originator of salaries of $5 per day for workers (which was considered a good wage at that time) as well as the creator of the 40-hour working week.

Ford would continue to develop trucks. The Model TT truck, produced in 1917, was Ford's first venture into the big-rig market. With its solid rubber tyres, wood-spoked wheels and canvas tarpaulin, the first Model TT wasn't much to look at. But later versions, with carved wood panelled bodies, solid roofs, electric lights, pneumatic tyres and glass windscreens, would substantially improve the TT's overall looks and saleability. The first TT was powered by a 2898cc (177ci) engine (positioned over the front axle and in front of the driver, 'conventional' style) with three-speed transmission. The truck chassis, though modelled on the Model T, had a longer and sturdier frame. The wheelbase was also 61cm (2ft) longer and the Model TT had a stiffer rear suspension than the Model T did.

### Ford creates modern assembly line

As he'd done with his other vehicles, Ford immediately put his assembly-line magic to work for the Ford Model TT. No less than 25 Model TT truck chassis rolled off the production line each day. By 1922, the number of trucks produced by Ford per day had grown to 193,294 units, a testimony to Ford's ability to survive the war's end, thanks to the fact the company continued to produce civilian vehicles throughout the war. In short, while the war in Europe had ultimately meant the end of companies that had over-invested in wartime truck production, it had only helped increase Ford's truck sales abroad and at home.

The Depression years that followed had their effect, with Ford truck sales falling just like everyone else's. Still, thanks to Ford's light truck business and the affordability of its vehicles, its sales remained healthier than most. What finally brought full recovery to the company was Ford's introduction of the Flathead (a.k.a. L-head) V-8 engine in 1932. The engine would be offered in all the company's truck models as well as its cars.

### Introduction of V-8

Ford engineers cut corners by casting the engine in a single piece rather than several. By doing so they also reduced the number of engine parts, which increased durability (but also made it harder to repair). The end result was that the V-8 engine boosted Ford truck and car sales and re-established the company as the industry leader.

Inset: *Simplicity was the keynote of Ford's design, exemplified by its single transverse front spring. The TT was cheap to buy and cheap to maintain.*

## Specifications

**Country:** USA
**Year manufactured from:** 1917
**Engine:** petrol powered
**Transmission:** two-speed
**Payload:** 1.016 tonne (one ton)
**Applications:** delivery
**Special features:** later versions included electric lights, pneumatic tyres, etc.

Below: *One of the TT's strengths was its adaptability to a host of different special duties, such as this dumper truck for small consignments of building materials.*

LIBERTY

1918 USA

# LIBERTY CLASS B

The Liberty Class B was designed by a committee of American military officials, members of the American Society of Automotive Engineers and volunteers from 45 American manufacturers.

The Liberty concept was born, like most other inventions, out of necessity. The Allied forces in Europe were having a hard time maintaining and repairing their trucks during World War I. American military officials soon realized that military trucks made of standardized and interchangeable parts would improve their situation.

## Standard design

Specs for the standard Liberty Class B, 4x2, 3.04-tonne (3-ton) truck were submitted to US Army officials in July 1917, and a design committee was formed. By October 1917, two prototype trucks had been built and were available for testing. (The engine block was made by Continental, its cylinder heads by Waukesha and its pistons by Hercules.) The trials proved so successful that by mid-November, the US government had already signed contracts for the manufacture of the Liberty B's standardized components.

The final Standard B 5.08-tonne (5-ton) would be 6.6m (21ft 9in) long by 2.1m (7ft) wide and 1.9m (6ft 3in) high. It would have four forward and one reverse gear, a 4.07m (160.5in) wheelbase and front tyres that were smaller than the rear ones.The truck's L-head engine would measure 255cc (425ci) and run four cycles, with 38.7kw (52bhp). Production of the Standard B Liberty truck would begin in April 1918.

Above: *The need to standardise military trucks to simplify spare part supplies and maintenance led to the Liberty which was built by a number of US manufacturers from 1918.*

## Specifications

**Country:** USA
**Year manufactured from:** 1918
**Engine:** petrol powered
**Transmission:** four-speed transmission, low gear reduction
**Payload:** 3.04 tonnes (three tons)
**Applications:** military
**Special features:** produced by multiple manufacturers for military

PIERCE ARROW TRUCK
**1920 USA**

# PIERCE ARROW

Pierce Arrow trucks built nearly 7000 of its cab-behind-engine trucks for export in 1918 alone. Their original truck had been a cab-over-engine design, but it didn't do well during testing so was abandoned.

Above: *Pierce Arrow of Buffalo, New York were one of the earliest truck builders to introduce worm drive axles when most other heavy trucks featured chain drive.*

## Specifications

**Country:** USA
**Year manufactured from:** 1920
**Engine:** dual valve petrol powered
**Transmission:** worm drive
**Payload:** not available
**Applications:** multiple
**Special features:** dual ignition, shockproof windscreen glass and back up lights

The massive demand for Pierce Arrows overseas would make it one of the most respected truck makers in North America at that time, ranked alongside Packard and Alco in terms of quality and expense. The period following the war was bad for truck makers in that demand was way down, but good in that the US government had finally realized the importance of road building.

The United States Army had made its first transcontinental road trip from Washington, D.C. to San Francisco, California, in 1919, in part to encourage the Government to invest in a national interstate road system for defence purposes, and Dwight D. Eisenhower, a Captain in the Army at that time, went along for the ride. After 62 days of treacherous travel on dirt roads and crumbling bridges, Eisenhower and his contemporaries were convinced better roads were the answer. The government would subsequently shell out $75 million on road building and improvements.

### Fifth wheel standardized

Truck manufacturers were ready with improvements of their own. The fifth wheel was patented and became standardized on trucks in 1920. Backup lights were standard by 1922, and shockproof glass was used in windscreens by 1926. But Pierce Arrow was ahead of the pack as usual, as their 1920 truck already had all of these features. It also had dual ignition and a dual-valved engine for more power and better fuel economy. And it could also be hooked up to different trailers.

HUG

1922 USA

# HUG MODEL T

In 1921, Hug decided to build its own trucks to suit its business specifications. Rugged but reliable, the Hug truck range was used during the twenties and the thirties for the big American construction projects.

Left: *The Hug Model T was a 'no frills' machine built along simple rugged lines and aimed at the construction industry.*

With its open cab and its simple design, the Model T was a rugged lorry designed for heavy applications. It was fitted with a Buda 25kW (34hp) petrol engine and a Warner three-speed transmission with a Clark spiral bevel axle, as well as two-wheel brakes. The top speed was about 72km/h (45mph), double the speed of many other trucks from the same period. The rubber tyres, with dual rear tyres, were uncommon for a severe-duty truck and despite a small size the Model T could carry a load of up 2.03 tonnes (2 tons). It was bodied with a dump or with a concrete mixer. In the middle of the twenties, three other models were built, with payloads from 1.52 to 3.56 tonnes (1½ tons to 3½ tons). Like all the Hug trucks until 1932, they were powered by Buda engines. Hug used subcontractor-built components like Clark, Columbia, Timken or Wisconsin axles and Brown-Lipe or Fuller transmissions. These trucks kept the rugged, 'no-frills' appearance, and in 1927 a massive six-tonner with a seven-speed gearbox appeared. After 1930, the range was completed with the 'Roadbuilder' series and, for the first time, the series was available with Caterpillar diesel engines. At the beginning of the war, Hug manufactured some 6x6 military trucks, but no contracts were concluded and 1942 was the last production year for the company.

## Specifications

**Country:** USA
**Year manufactured from:** 1922
**Engine:** four cylinder Buda engine, 25kw (34hp)
**Transmission:** three-speed
**Payload:** 2.03 tonnes (two tons)
**Applications:** dump truck, concrete mixer
**Special features:** rubber tyres, open cab

CHENARD AND WALCKER

**Mid 1920s France**

# CHENARD & WALCKER

For most people, Chenard & Walcker was a car manufacturer. However, it was also an innovative truck builder. In France, its contribution to the semi-trailer combination was significant.

Above: *The Chenard & Walcker UT was one of the first tractors ever built.*

## Specifications

**Country:** France

**Year manufactured from:** 1927

**Engine:** four cylinder petrol powered, 15kW (20hp)

**Transmission:** three-speed

**Payload:** two to ten tonnes (1.96 to 9.84 tons)

**Applications:** semi-trailer or trailer hauling

**Special features:** short wheelbase truck, trailer coupling system

The prestigious Chenard & Walcker company was founded in France in 1901 and was famous for its cars. In 1920, the company was the fourth-largest car manufacturer in the country.

### FAR company

At the end of the Great War, the company created a new department, the FAR company, in order to exploit the patented Lagache et Glazsmann trailer-coupling system. Their trailers and semi-trailers initially had a very limited distribution, and it was not until the sixties that they spread throughout Europe. Chenard & Walcker wanted to prove that a small short-wheelbase tractor could haul more payload than a rigid truck on short distances. The tractor could haul a trailer to a warehouse, uncouple the trailer while it was unloaded, and return to base for a further haul. This system was more profitable than using a rigid truck. The company built two- or three-axle bonneted tractors. Some heavy 6x4 axle configurations, with chain drive, were designed for logging applications or special big haulages. Some of them were sold as omnibus tractor units in Holland.

INTERNATIONAL HARVESTER
**1928 USA**

# INTERNATIONAL HARVESTER SIX-SPEED SPECIAL

By 1928, the International Harvester Company (IHC) of America had already established a name for its trucks, and not just back in rural America, but also for multiple applications in cities.

International Harvester trucks were being sold in countries as far away as Japan, where IHC chassis were marketed for multiple applications, including commercial hauling, municipal work and passenger transportation. Commercial hauliers were available in sizes from 1360.5kg to 4535kg (3000 to 10,000lb) payload capacity, with Speed Truck light- to medium-duty vehicles in 1.27-, 1.52-, 2.03- and 3.04- tonne (1¼-, 1½-, 2- and 3-ton) versions and heavy-duty trucks in 2.54-, 3.55- and 5.08- tonne 2½-, 3½- and 5-ton models. They could be fitted with express bodies, panel bodies, dump bodies with an under-body hoist, and special bodies for any purpose. For municipal work, they could be fitted as fire trucks, dustcarts, ambulances, police wagons, street maintenance vehicles, etc. For passenger transportation the sky was the limit.

Above: *Launched in 1928, International's 'Six Speed Special' one-tonner featured a two-speed rear axle which, combined with the normal three-speed gearbox, provided six forward and two reverse ratios.*

## Six-speeder returns to roots

The International Harvester Six-Speed Special truck, introduced in 1928, was the company's first truck with a two-speed rear axle (for going in reverse – the truck also had six speeds going forward.) It was specially designed for off-road rural haulage and became popular immediately. (In fact, earlier versions of the Six-Speed Special had already contributed to doubling International Harvester truck sales in the last three years.)

The Six-Speed Special owed at least some of its popularity to the fact that it was a return to the company's farming roots (IHC had started out producing one of North American's first motorized reapers.) But the Six-Speed Special double reverse wasn't the sole contributor to the company's success.

## Marketing goldmine

In 1928, IHC management hit on an idea that would become a tried-and-true truck-marketing goldmine thereafter – in the age of America's love affair with the romance of the desert (Howard Carter had discovered Tutankhamun's tomb in 1922) why not promote a truck used by someone who had conquered it? The idea soon paid off, in the form of an article/advertisement in the pages of the October 1928 edition of *Scientific American*.

The article, with the hero/explorer in the foreground and an International half-ton panel truck in the back, told the story of Sir Charles Markham and Baron Frederick Von Blixen-Fineke's 4828km (3000-mile) trek through the Sahara desert in the world's first four-wheel truck to do so. The truck had a fully covered cab and body, with unglazed windows on all sides to allow the desert air to circulate more freely (although as one would expect there was a system for covering the windows in case of sandstorms). It had an engine in front, and remountable pneumatic tyres (as well as several spares fastened to the body) and appeared to have been tough enough to endure the extreme temperatures and sand of the world's biggest desert.

The article describes in detail a first-person account of the journey made by Sir Charles Markham, of course it does not say whether the truck suffered from any mechanical problems along the way.

## Specifications

**Country:** USA
**Year manufactured from:** 1928
**Engine:** petrol powered
**Transmission:** six-speeds forward, two-speeds reverse
**Payload:** up to 5.08 tonnes (five tons)
**Applications:** multiple
**Special features:** specially designed for off road haulage

Left: *With its roots in the agricultural industry, International Harvester produced tough trucks that were highly popular among farmers who often needed to traverse unmade roads.*

REO SPEED WAGON
⚒ **1929 USA**

# REO SPEED WAGON STANDARD 1½-TONNER

The REO Speed Wagon was named after its designer, Ransom Eli Olds (1864–1950), who founded the Olds Motor Vehicle Company in Lansing, Michigan, in 1897 and later the REO Motor Company.

One of his most popular vehicles, the REO Speed Wagon (from which a popular rock group of the 1970s later took its name) was originally fitted out as flatbed pick-up truck. It was very high speed and heavy duty and was considered a milestone of transportation history. Its rugged ability to withstand the rough roads of North America in the early 1900s meant it would eventually be developed to service multiple applications. Over the years it would see service as a tow truck, fire truck, fuel delivery truck, indeed, for all applications that required a rugged workhorse design.

Indeed, advertisements for the truck in the 1920s boasted 'This REO Speed Wagon fits every business… Even in those lines where you would naturally think only in terms of 10-ton trucks, we find Speed Wagons rendering splendid – and owners tell – more economical….'

REOs (cars included) were popular all the way up to the time of the Great Depression, and were reportedly capable of logging 160,930km (100,000) miles without abnormal wear and tear. Fans claim the

Above: *Reo first adopted the 'Speed Wagon' name for its trucks in 1915 and progressively updated the range through to 1939 when the last Speed Wagons were built. This is a late 1930s two/three-tonner with tipping body.*

Speed Wagon set the standard that most companies producing trucks at that time tried to imitate.

The first REO Speed Wagon was a ¾-tonner. It was advertised as being capable of up to 35.4km/h (22mph) – although those who used it claimed it could reach 64.3km/h (40mph) – even when fully loaded. The Speed Wagon had an electric starter and a 33.5kw (45hp), four-cylinder engine. It also had a 13-plate clutch and three-speed selective sliding gear transmission and bevel drive.

## Several models available

By the end of the 'Roaring Twenties' the Speed Wagon chassis was available in several models, including the Junior ½-ton, the Tonner, the Standard 1½-ton with two choices of wheelbase, the Master (2 tons), and the Heavy Duty (3 tons).

The 1929 Speed Wagon had a six-cylinder engine, with L-type head, 8.2cm (3.25in) bore, and 10.1cm (4in) stroke. It had four-point suspension, seven-bearing crankshaft, and aluminium alloy pistons. It also had a thermostatic temperature control, semi-automatic spark control and a single-plate clutch. As was usual at that time, the chassis could be fitted out with a coupe cab (or not) and there were three standard body styles available, full panel, stake (wood panel flatbed) or Express (with or without a canopy top). The vehicle rode on spoked, malleable iron artillery wheels and pneumatic tyres, with a suspension that included extra-long semi-elliptical springs. Speed Wagons of the time also had four wheel internal hydraulic brakes, a standard 58cm (23in) wheelbase and an irreversible steering gear, not to mention an automatic chassis oiling system.

But more than that, Olds' Speed Wagon trucks were popular for their stylish designs, as well, not to mention the backing of the familiar Olds name. At its height in the 1920s, the factory in Lansing, Michigan employed about 6000 people.

## Customer testimonials

By 1930, testimonials alone would sell the trucks: 'It might interest you to know that my second two-ton REO Speed Wagon has passed the 65,000-mile mark with a repair expense of but $201.10, and I expect to run it another 66,000 miles', reads a customer testimonial published in 1930. REO stopped making cars altogether in 1936 and changed hands several times starting in the 1950s, eventually merging with the Diamond T division of the Cleveland-based White Motor Company.

## Specifications

**Country:** USA
**Year manufactured from:** 1929
**Engine:** four cylinder
**Transmission:** three-speed selective sliding
**Payload:** 0.76 tonnes (¾ ton)
**Applications:** delivery
**Special features:** electric starter

Below: *The Speed Wagon was ruggedly built from the beginning and boasted powerful performance. A variety of body types for different applications was available.*

DELAHAYE

**1929 France**

# DELAHAYE PS 92

Delayahe was one of Europe's most advanced car manufacturers at the beginning of the 20th century. The company was founded in Tours, but quickly re-established itself in Paris under Emile Delahaye.

The company was famous for fire engines and fire apparatus. Hence the major part of Delayahe's income was the truck business, especially during World War I. Delahaye became renowned for its beautiful engines: all the Delayahe engines were fast and powerful – exactly what a fire truck needed when a rapid response was required.

## PS 92

After World War I, Delayahe brought the fire engine and fire truck ranges up to date. The best example of this modernization is the PS 92. The Premier Secours Model 92 ('First Aid' fire truck) was very popular in all French rural districts until the fifties. This fire engine was smaller than previous models, but had an improved practicality. In many ways it was a thoroughly modern fire truck, with a pump driven by the engine (called 'Petit cheval', i.e. 'Little Horse'), a 3182-litre (700-gallon) water supply, an independent hose reel and a six-man crew. It had a 30kw (40hp) four-cylinder engine, but the radiator size was increased to avoid overheating when the pump was being operated.

Above: *The Delahaye PS 92 was one of the early fire trucks produced in France.*

## Specifications

**Country:** France
**Year manufactured from:** 1929
**Engine:** four cylinders overhead valves engine, 30 kw (40hp)
**Transmission:** not available
**Payload:** not applicable
**Applications:** fire engine
**Special features:** engine driven pump

BERLIET
**1930 France**

# BERLIET DIESEL-POWERED TRUCK

Marius Berliet started experimenting with automobiles in 1894. His first car was built in a shed. Because he had to be able to get it out through the garden gate, it could only be as wide as that.

Above: *Berliet introduced its first diesel engines in 1930. They were of the indirect injection type.*

## Specifications

**Country:** France
**Year manufactured from:** 1930
**Engine:** diesel powered Martin
**Transmission:** chain drive
**Payload:** not available
**Applications:** ideal for long haul
**Special features:** France's first diesel-powered truck

Berliet produced his first truck, for a silk manufacturer, in 1897. The first trucks were built on car chassis, but they mounted some of the biggest engines of the time – as much as 59.6kw (80hp). They were also forward control. Berliet eventually received the ultimate recognition as a truck maker, producing 40 CBA trucks per day for the French military during the battle of Verdun in 1916. In 1917, both Berliet and Renault produced a tank specifically ordered by the French government, known as 'the Diamond brand'. During the war, Berliet produced up to 16 of these tanks per day at its plant in Venisseux.

### Introduction of diesel-powered trucks

Berliet introduced France's first diesel-powered truck in 1930. It had a Martin diesel engine (Martin was a French manufacturer that had produced its first diesel engine in 1928). The new engine certainly stimulated sales, as diesel was much less expensive and easier to maintain than petrol. It also proved more powerful – ideal for the long-distance transportation of goods.

BEDFORD
⚒ **1930s UK**

# BEDFORD 'W' SERIES

In Bedford nomenclature the first letter indicates model. According to some historians, the 'W' denotes a chassis made to wartime specifications, although the 'W' series reportedly came out in the early 1930s.

Above: *The English company Vauxhall Motors started producing the Bedford brand of trucks in the early 1930s. The first trucks of the 'W' series were four-wheelers.*

Bedford was a subsidiary company of Vauxhall Motors, which was a well-known provider of commercial vehicles for the United Kingdom and export markets. It began as the Vauxhall Iron Works, founded by Alexander Wilson in 1857. The company originally built machinery such as pumps and engines for the marine industry. It was named Vauxhall because it was first located in Wandsworth Road, in Vauxhall, London.

By the turn of the century Wilson had left the business and the remaining board directors became interested in starting production of a 'horseless carriage'. The company had already started producing a petrol-powered launch (one of the first in marine engineering). In 1903, the company was manufacturing a 3.7kw (5hp) single-cylinder car, available to the public for 130 guineas.

The vehicle sold well, and the board of directors decided to expand the production of petrol-powered vehicles. But in order to do so, the factory would have to move out of London. The company acquired a site in Luton, Bedfordshire, where it moved in 1905. The company continued to do business under the name Vauxhall Iron Works until 1907, when the modern name of Vauxhall Motors Ltd. and the company's griffin emblem was adopted.

Car production continued. Then, in November 1925 Vauxhall was acquired by General Motors. Chevrolet trucks had been on sale in Britain since 1923, but were costly owing to import tax. In 1925 GM set up an operation at Hendon to prepare imported vehicles and introduced Buick, Cadillac, Chevrolet, La Salle, Marquette, Oakland, Oldsmobile and Pontiac cars, as well as Chevrolet and GMC trucks.

But with the country in the grip of a worldwide Depression, there was no little public hostility to imported products. (Over two million people were unemployed in the United Kingdom alone at this time.) So General Motors decided to camouflage its foreign roots by building a completely 'British' truck using Vauxhall's Luton plant.

## The British truck is born

By the early 1930s, assembly of the last Chevrolet and GMC trucks and vans in Britain had ended and the manufacture of Bedford trucks had begun. In 1930, the first true Bedford was on the road.

The first trucks of the 'W' series were four-wheelers – a 30cwt truck and a 2.03-tonne (2-ton) version. The trucks were probably equipped with Bedford's own four- or six-cylinder petrol-powered engines, which could produce up to 20.1kw (27hp).

The earliest 'W' model trucks most probably had four-speed gearboxes attached to bevel drives on the rear axles. It is also safe to assume they had Dewandre servo brakes – as those would also appear on the company's commercial passenger vehicles at that time.

The trucks proved so successful that by 1937 sales of the Bedford 'W' series had reached 30,000.

## 'W' series on hold

Historians report the 'W' series was put on hold during World War II, when the production of civilian and commercial vehicles in Britain was suspended in favour of focusing the nation's efforts on the manufacture of military vehicles. Bedford trucks manufactured during World War II included the 'MW' and 'OY' types, with modified tractors. Bedford also produced the 'QL' 4x4 for military use. After World War II, commercial and civilian production would resume, and Bedford would resurrect many of the elements of the original 'W' series.

## Specifications

**Country:** UK

**Year manufactured from:** 1931

**Engine:** four or six cylinder petrol powered

**Transmission:** four-speed, bevel axle

**Payload:** up to 2.03 tonnes (two tons)

**Applications:** delivery, military

**Special features:** servo brakes

Below: *Built in Luton, England by Vauxhall Motors, Bedford trucks dominated the UK medium truck market in the 1930s. Vauxhall Motors went on to be a major supplier of military trucks during World War II.*

GMC

🛠 **1930s USA**

# GMC HEAVY-DUTY TRUCKS

By the early 1930s, GMC trucks were available with payload capacities of up to 13.6 tonnes (15 tons). Unlike their colleagues at Chevrolet, GMC engineers were focusing on designing heavy-duty trucks.

## Specifications

**Country:** USA
**Year manufactured from:** 1930s
**Engine:** six cylinder, petrol powered
**Transmission:** five-speed, over and under drive
**Payload:** up to 15.2 tonnes (15 tons)
**Applications:** multiple
**Special features:** first sleeper cab optional

Tandem rear axles were already available on trucks like the 10-tonner T0-956 prior to 1933. And by 1933, GMC had fitted its first sleeper cab on a heavy-duty truck, showing the company had a pretty good sense of where trucking was going in terms of long haul. The same year saw downdraft carburettors as well as overhead valve engines adopted in the company's 2-tonner series.

By that time, GMC's heavy-duty trucks were coming standard with 11.6-litre (707ci) six-cylinder engines rated at 12.9kw (173hp). The engine used twin-plate clutches and had a five-speed transmission, with both over and under drive. Chain drive or worm drive was the standard on the tandem axles. And for the heaviest trucks, air brakes made by Westinghouse were standard as well. A six-cylinder, 52.2kw (70hp) side-valve engine, or the larger 89.5kw (120hp) overhead-valve six-cylinder engine were available for trucks with a payload capacity greater than 1.52 tonnes (1.5 tons) in 1934.

### Streamlined design

The company redesigned their cabs in 1935, making even the heaviest-duty truck cabs more streamlined. Hydraulic brakes were also added, with full air actuation for the heaviest trucks and hydrovac for medium duty. By 1937, the company had 12 conventional models and 11 cab-over-engine models in its heavy-duty truck line. Diesel engines were standard for the 2.03-to 6.1-tonne (2- to 6-ton) range by 1939, unlike similar models built by Chevrolet.

Above: *GMC heavy trucks of the early 1930s were of very staid appearance but from 1936 onwards the company adopted a more streamlined approach with stylish radiator grilles and sloping 'vee'd' windscreens.*

GENERAL MOTORS
**1936 Germany**

# OPEL BLITZ

General Motors acquired the German motor company Opel AG in 1929. The Opel Blitz was the result of this venture, but with the rise of the Third Reich, the German government decided to nationalize the company.

## Specifications

**Country:** Germany
**Year manufactured from:** 1936
**Engine:** four cylinder petrol engine, 50 kw (68hp)
**Transmission:** not available
**Payload:** three tonnes (2.95 tons)
**Applications:** general purpose military truck
**Special features:** 4x2 'S' Type, 4x4 'A' Type, Half Track 'Maultier' Type

Above: *Just as General Motors acquired Vauxhall in the UK so it did Opel in Germany. During World War II Opel Blitz military trucks were widely used by the German army.*

More than 100,000 Opel Blitz ('Lightning') were built during World War II. The figure is far from the 800,000 GMC 6x6, but the Blitz was at first planned as a civilian commercial truck. This light vehicle was born in 1931 with a 3.6-litre (220-cu.in) Buick engine (Buick was part of General Motors). The first series had a 1.75-tonne (1.72-ton) payload, which then increased to 2.5 tonnes (2.46 tons) and finally 3 tonnes (2.95 tons) with the most famous Blitz, known as the 'S' type. This model made its initial test in 1936 and looked modern with its steel cabin. The petrol engine was far superior to any of its diesel competitors. After several testings, the Blitz was chosen by the German army. It could accept more than the mentioned payload and its ability to go where no other two-wheel-drive truck could go is legendary.

### Variants

In 1940, Opel built a second version, a 4x4 truck known as the 'A' type. About 25,000 of this cross-country Blitz were made and another half-track model was derived from the original frame, codenamed 'Maultier' ('Mule') – only 4,000 entered production from 1942, and most were sent to the Russian front. The Blitz was able to accept lots of bodies: ambulances, tankers, radio-trucks and general-purpose.

VOLVO
1931 Sweden

# VOLVO LV66

With the LV 66, the Swedish Volvo company definitively entered the truck market. This truck was indeed a completely new commercial vehicle, designed to compete with the other local truck builder, Scania-Vabis.

Until the beginning of the thirties, Volvo used some car parts in the construction of their lorries. However, as they began considering increasing the payload of their vehicles, the Volvo managers Assar Gabrielsson and Gustaf Larson decided to launch a larger truck with heavy components.

## Power problems

From its first appearance on a drawing board, the new truck had to choose between a six inline or an eight inline cylinder engine with overhead or flathead valves. Finally, a six inline overhead valves engine was chosen. The petrol-powered DC 75 engine offered 56kw (75hp) and ran in combination with a new four-speed gearbox. The new LV 66 and 68 ranges were sold from 1931. Different wheelbases and two- or three-axle configurations (from 1933) were available. For the first time, Volvo was also able to sell with a single or a double reduction. In 1933, these ranges could be powered by a new engine, the 'Hesselman' engine, based on the petrol engine, but which could run on diesel fuel thanks to a mechanical injection system. The LV 66 and 68 series were quite popular, and produced reasonable sales figures, but as three-axle trucks or as heavy-duty vehicles, the Volvo DC 75 engine wasn't powerful enough.

Above: *The LV66 took Volvo into a heavier weight class in 1931.*

## Specifications

**Country:** Sweden
**Year manufactured from:** 1931
**Engine:** six cylinder petrol powered, 56kw (75hp)
**Transmission:** not available
**Payload:** 3.5 tonnes (3.4 tons)
**Applications:** delivery truck, tanker, dump truck
**Special features:** first real Volvo truck, new engine DC 75, new gearbox and new axle configuration

KENWORTH

mid 1930s USA

# KENWORTH 516 'BUBBLENOSE'

Kenworth unveiled its first cab-over-engine design, the 'Bubblenose', in 1936. The truck was designed with a shortened nose to provide maximum payload while complying with the overall state truck length limits.

Above: *Length limits imposed in some states during 1935 led to an increase in cab-over-engine trucks. Typical of the era was the Kenworth 516 'Bubblenose' 6-wheel truck seen here with a drawbar trailer.*

## Specifications

**Country:** USA
**Year manufactured from:** mid -1930s
**Engine:** four or six cylinder petrol powered, four cylinder diesel powered
**Transmission:** five-speed
**Payload:** up to 3.6 tonnes (four tons)
**Applications:** multiple
**Special features:** chrome grille

Weight restrictions had also been imposed by the Motor Carrier Act in 1935, so Kenworth had also begun building its own cabs from sheet metal. Chrome was also an aesthetic element in the overall Kenworth design; the trucks were instantly recognizable thanks to their chrome grille.

Kenworth partner Harry Kent would not live to enjoy the new design's success. In 1937, he died of a heart attack. Nevertheless, Kent's legacy of cost-cutting and manufacturing efficiencies would continue, resulting in Kenworth becoming increasingly successful over the next three years.

## Ten truck models

Among them would be 10 models of trucks, including the 2.03-tonne (2-ton) Model 88, powered by an 61.9kw (83hp) Hercules JXC engine and the 7-tonner Model 241C powered by a 93.2kw (125hp) six-cylinder Cummins diesel engine. Buda and Herschell-Spillman petrol engines were also available for the 4-tonner model 146B and the 7.1-tonne (7-ton) Model 241A. (All petrol engines had six cylinders by 1937.) The 505, 506 and 507 models were powered by Cummins four-cylinder diesel engines.

Kenworth also got into bus production at the end of the 1930s The company custom-built the canvas-topped Tri-Coach bus, which could carry 18 passengers, for the Rainier National Park Company. Five of them were delivered to Rainier in 1938. Small buses were also produced. But truck production would continue to be Kenworth's focus, with at least 17 six-wheeled truck models available by 1940.

ERF
1937 UK

# ERF OE4

The ERF OE4 weighed only 2.72 tonnes (3 tons) unloaded, but was capable of hauling a 5.4-tonnes (6-ton) payload. It had a frame which swept up over the rear axle.

## Specifications

**Country:** UK
**Year manufactured from:** 1937
**Engine:** four cylinder diesel
**Transmission:** five-speed
**Payload:** 6.1 tonnes (six tons)
**Applications:** multiple
**Special features:** could haul twice its weight unloaded

Above: *The OE4 was ERF's lightest truck and was powered by a Gardner 4LK diesel which boasted excellent fuel economy.*

The OE4 had other distinctive design elements as well, thanks to the ingenuity of its designer Ernest Sherratt. The stylish grille was positioned in front of the radiator so as to conceal it. This look was very modern for its time and it would be used for many future ERF trucks in years to come.

The Gardner diesel engine would be used to power the small but powerful OE4. In the late 1930s, Gardner would introduce its 3.8-litre (230.6ci) four-cylinder 4LK diesel engine, capable of up to 42.5kw (57hp) at 2100rpm. The light power unit, with matching transmission, was ideal for the ERF OE4.

By the beginning of 1939, an estimated 40 ERF trucks were rolling off the production line every month. But six months later, World War II would have its effect on industrial production in the UK.

### Design innovation continues

The company did, nevertheless introduce a few new vehicles at the start of the war, including its 6.8-tonne (7.5-ton) tipper truck. Engineer Ernest Sherratt designed the truck with two goals in mind: weight reduction and low body floor height. Weight was strictly controlled by careful selection and integration of parts.

FODEN

1937 UK

# FODEN DG RANGE

It would take time to convince Foden's conservative board members that diesel power would overtake steamers. Several company officials were believers, among them E.R. Foden, his son Dennis and brother William.

Above: *In 1937 Foden brought out its DG range, powered by Gardner LW series diesel engines with four, five or six cylinders.*

## Specifications

**Country:** UK
**Year manufactured from:** 1937
**Engine:** diesel powered, four to six cylinder Gardner
**Transmission:** five-speed worm drive
**Payload:** variable
**Applications:** delivery, then heavy duty
**Special features:** first Foden diesel

Eventually, E.R. Foden was forced to resign. To Foden's eternal regret, E.R. founded ERF and in June 1933 brought out the diesel-powered C-14, which made the nascent company an almost instant success.

ERF's success and the fact that insurers were increasingly reluctant to insure steam boilers, finally convinced Foden board members that the internal combustion engine was in fact necessary to the survival of company's commercial vehicle line. Thanks to some of the company's more forward thinkers, Foden had already begun experimenting with petrol-driven vehicles. Foden then used several petrol engines before focusing on diesel lorries such as the R and S-types.

## DG range

Finally the company convinced William Foden to return from Australia. His return heralded the production of the company's first diesel trucks and turned the company's fortunes around. In 1937 Foden brought out its DG range, powered by Gardner LW series diesel engines with four, five or six cylinders and with a capacity of 1.4 litres (23ci). Foden first used these engines in lorries, but their use in heavy-duty commercial vehicles such as ballasted drawbar tractors followed.

FWD

1937 USA

# FWD COEs

According to some truck historians, FWD was the first North American truck manufacturer to introduce the cab-over-engine design to its commercial vehicle range.

Left: *In 1937, FWD brought out a COE cab with a two-piece V-shaped windscreen. It would be followed by the four-door COE crew cab. Soon COEs would be available in a wide variety of shapes and sizes, even on 6x4s.*

The company had its start in 1910, when Otto Zachow, a machinist in Clintonville, Wisconsin, patented a double-Y universal joint in a ball and socket. Zachow's U-joint allowed for the wheels of a vehicle to rotate and be steered simultaneously. With the help of his brother-in-law William Besserdich, who was also a machinist, Otto subsequently built a steam-powered passenger car, which used the new U-joints on its axles.

The steamer wasn't much of a success, so the brothers-in-law turned their hands to petrol-driven vehicles. Their very first, nicknamed the Battleship, weighed 1723.3kg (3800lb). But the brothers still had no intention of getting into automotive manufacture. They just used the vehicle to demonstrate their U-joints. Finally, a group of investors managed to encourage the brothers-in-law to start their own company building four-wheel-drive vehicles. The Four Wheel Drive Automotive Company (FWD) was founded in 1909.

## FWD dominates military production

World War I proved profitable for FWD, with the American military ordering so many FWD trucks that other manufacturers were given special licenses to build them as well. Post-war, with half the market flooded with FWD trucks, the company would get by selling spare parts for their maintenance.

Through the 1920s the company made several improvements to its truck line, including introducing pneumatic tyres as standard equipment on trucks like the Model B, which had been produced since 1918. The company also focused on building special-purpose trucks, for fire services, utilities, oil hauling etc.

By the mid-1930s, FWD had innovated further – expanding its product range in terms of payload capacity and powerplants. In 1937, FWD brought out a COE cab with a two-piece V-shaped windscreen. It would be followed by the four-door COE crew cab. Soon COEs would be available in a wide variety of shapes and sizes.

## Further innovations

FWD introduced new Cummins diesel powerplants as well as double-reduction or multiple-geared axles. With a short wheelbase and a shorter frame than a conventional truck, the COE series could maximize the payload capacity with a longer body or a longer trailer. But the drawback of such a cabin was the engine inside the driver's less roomy cab. The noise, the heat and the burned-oil smell were rather uncomfortable, especially during the summer. FWD trucks retained the old-style front cabin during the thirties and didn't keep up with the 'streamlined' fashions. However, the trucks were mainly used in severe-application duties and the aerodynamic design was secondary. During World War II, FMW supplied the US forces with military trucks. The SU heavy model was built as a COE or Conventional model for the US Marine Corps, and for the Red Army and British forces for use as an artillery tractor It was powered by a 86kw (115hp) Waukesha petrol engine and could carry up to 5.08/6.1 tonnes (5/6 tons).

## Post-war cabs

After the war, the company used a new cabin built by International, then a Dodge cab was fitted on the new Tractioneer series introduced in 1958. The company also developed custom-designed trucks to utilize Seagrave fire apparatus.

## Specifications

**Country:** USA
**Year manufactured from:** 1937
**Engine:** variable
**Transmission:** five-speed and worm drive
**Payload:** variable
**Applications:** multiple
**Special features:** two piece V-shaped windscreen

Left: *FWD SU COE all-wheel-drive trucks came into their own as military vehicles in World War II.*

FORD

1930s USA

# FORD V-8 MODEL BB

In 1932, the new Ford V-8 caused a sensation because it was reliable, smooth and powerful and had a low-cost flathead engine. It powered the new 'BB' type commercial truck chassis that superseded the 'AA' types.

The 'Flathead' Ford V-8 engine immediately became a success, despite initial casting troubles and overheating problems. With a cast-in-one piece, it had a 90 degree arrangement with a 3.6-litre (221-ci) displacement for 48kw (65hp). It wasn't really sophisticated, but Ford could offer eight cylinders for a price that no other manufacturer could. The new BB type truck was offered in 334cm (131½in) and 398cm (157in) wheelbase with a new heftier steel frame. The semi-elliptic springs, an underseat fuel tank and a revised shaft drive were fitted too. Despite the revolutionary engine, the Great Depression didn't help sales and Ford had to face up to million dollar losses. But the fleet operators were very enthusiastic about the V-8 trucks, with their 'V-8' logos proudly fixed to the front grille, and in 1934 the engine was improved with a new counterbalanced cast-alloy steel crankshaft which contributed to increase smoothness by reducing vibrations. A new dual-downdraft Stromberg carburettor was fitted too and at this time. In 1935, a new body shell was launched and the revised frame changed the name of the truck series. The 'BB' type was phased out to become the Model 51.

Above: *There's no doubt about the engine – the 'V-8' logo on the grille is clearly displayed.*

## Specifications

**Country:** USA

**Year manufactured from:** 1932

**Engine:** eight V cylinders, petrol powered, 48kw (65hp)

**Transmission:** three gears

**Payload:** 1.5 tonnes (1.52 tons)

**Applications:** stake body, delivery truck, tanker, platform, dump truck

**Special features:** new V-8 engine

AUSTIN

1939 UK

# AUSTIN K2

In 1939 the Birmingham-based Austin company entered the truck field with an extended range up to a 5.08-tonne (5-ton) payload capacity. The K2 was the most widely used truck.

Above: *Austin's new K range of light to medium trucks was first announced in 1939 but full production did not begin until after World War II.*

Right: *Such was the K model's similarity to its rival, the Luton-built Bedford, that it was nicknamed the 'Birmingham Bedford'.*

## Specifications

**Country:** UK
**Year manufactured from:** 1939
**Engine:** six cylinder petrol powered, 20kw (27hp)
**Transmission:** four-speed to bevel
**Payload:** 2.03 tonnes (two tons)
**Applications:** stake body, parcel delivery truck, dropside platform

The design of the Austin trucks was very similar to the Bedford trucks, and Austin was indeed nicknamed the 'Birmingham Bedford company'. The 2.03-tonne (2-ton) K2 was designed before World War II, but the civilian steel cab model didn't get underway until 1945. However, during the war about 13,000 K2/Y were built as military ambulances in Austin's Longbridge works.

### Post-war service

After the war, the K2 began a new career as delivery van, cattle truck or dropside wooden platform vehicle. The engine was a well-proven petrol six-cylinder rated at 20kw (27hp) with a four-speed gearbox. The Austin K2 and the bigger 5.08-tonne (5-ton) K4 were very popular on the British roads and they looked modern with a steel roof and a V-windscreen. In 1947, a new commercial vehicle entered the range: it was the Three Way Van K8 light truck, which became famous with its forward-control cab and its steel body. At the beginning of 1950, all the conventional K series had a facelift, with more modern bonnets and wings. But they were phased out when Austin merged with the British Motor Corporation in 1951.

SCAMMELL

1939–1940 UK

# SCAMMELL PIONEER MILITARY SERIES

The first Scammell articulated lorry was a 7.5-tonner built in 1921. From then on the company would focus mainly on building articulated and straight trucks with eight wheels.

In 1927, however, Scammell would come out with the Pioneer, a six-wheeled, off-road heavy-duty tractor with a rocking-type front axle and two feet of vertical movement at each rear wheel. The innovation made for incredible cross-country performance, which would make the Pioneer ideal for use in oil field and lumber operations.

With the outbreak of World War II, the Pioneer would also prove exceptionally useful for the British Army. The truck was used first as a tank transporter, but it would soon be put to other uses as well. The wartime Scammells were equipped with Gardner six-cylinder diesel engines which gave them the high torque at low speeds they needed for tank and truck recovery operations. And they were also ideal for towing the heavy pneumatic-tyred guns used at that time.

## Winch or crane

To move guns across ground or to recover stuck vehicles, the pioneer artillery tractor was fitted with a chassis winch in 1939, which could lift 8.1 tonnes (8 tons). The first 43 'breakdown' tractors, designated SV1S or SV1T, were also fitted with folding cranes.

Above: *The Scammell Pioneer's great strength was its exceptional off-road capability.*

## Specifications

**Country:** UK

**Year manufactured from:** 1939

**Engine:** six cylinder Gardner diesel

**Transmission:** five-speed

**Payload:** not available

**Applications:** heavy duty off road, military

**Special features:** 'breakdown' tractors fitted with folding cranes

PETERBILT
1939 USA

# PETERBILT 260GD

Peterbilt owed its beginnings to the California-based Fageol Truck Company, a truck maker that specialized in building trucks for the western US market.

Above: *Peterbilt adapted existing Fageol designs but achieved huge weight savings with extensive use of aluminium alloys.*

## Specifications

**Country:** USA
**Year manufactured from:** 1939
**Engine:** Cummins diesel powered
**Transmission:** four speed main and three auxiliary, double reduction at rear
**Payload:** not available
**Applications:** multiple
**Special features:** air brakes

Unfortunately, the Depression years would interfere with sales and Fageol would go into receivership in 1932. That was when T.A. Peterman, a lumberman from Washington, started worrying about where he could get good trucks. Peterman had been rebuilding surplus army trucks and modifying old logging trucks for use in his business. But by 1938, his lumber operations had expanded and he needed more trucks. He bought the old Fageol factory and started building custom chain-drive logging trucks in 1939. Of course, it would take some time for Peterman to truly figure out the ins and outs of truck making.

### Experiments with aluminium

For instance, the 1939 Model 260GD had an aluminium grille, which reduced weight but which also broke easily. Thus use of aluminium in the grille would be abandoned after just one year.

The engine proved more successful, however. It was an HB6 Cummins diesel that could develop up to 111.8kw (150hp), with a four-speed Brown-Lipe main transmission, as well as a three-speed auxiliary one. The 260GD also came equipped with a Timken double-reduction rear axle and air brakes.

As with most truck makers, Peterbilt's success or failure would depend largely on road development, industry and military needs during World War II. While Henry Ford was cranking out hundreds of trucks a day, Peterman set his sights on building 100 trucks a year, concentrating on quality, not quantity. Peterman succeeded building 14 units in 1939 and 82 in 1940.

FREIGHTLINER
🛠 **1940s USA**

# FREIGHTLINER CF100 COE

Freightliner trucks appear to be unique in early truck history in that they saw their beginnings in the hauling industry, rather than in engine or bicycle manufacturing.

Leyland James founded Consolidated Freightlines, a hauling company and the forerunner of Freightliner, in 1929 in Portland, Oregon. In true trucker tradition, James was always looking for ways to increase profit and payload. His appetite for finding new ways to do this, particularly when it came to technological innovation, was what led to the creation of Freightliner's very first trucks.

As usual, necessity was the mother of invention. When Leyland James wanted lighter trucks that could carry more payload and stay within the 18.3m (60ft) length limit required by most western US states, the suppliers he dealt with ignored him.

## Innovations in materials and design

So, with the help of mechanics already in his employ, James started adapting trucks himself. By the mid-1930s, James and his mechanics had already fitted some of his trucks with lighter aluminium parts, including brake shoes, suspension hanger brackets and trailer pulleys. Of course, aluminium truck and trailer bodies were the

Above: *Being in the tracking business, Leyland James of Consolidated Freightlines knew exactly what kind of track was required so he and his team went ahead and created the first Freightliner, the CF100.*

next logical step. Next came cab-over-engine designs, because by making the tractor shorter, James could increase the length of the trailer, thus increasing payload.

The very first Freightliner cab-over-engine design to hit the road for Consolidated Freightlines was assembled from spare parts and cabs welded together by Freightlines mechanics themselves. It was pulled together from a Fageol truck with a Truck and Coach Company chassis and a custom-designed Freightliner aluminium cab. It had a Cummins diesel engine, and it was a full ton lighter than any other design with a comparable payload.

James' cab-over-engine design proved so successful that the company would build 20 more over the next three years alone. Obviously, James' idea of making trucks lighter and trailers both lighter and longer was working.

## Expansion through the 1940s

By 1940, James had finally convinced other carriers, if not manufacturers, of the benefits of lighter, shorter truck designs to increase profits and payload. Consolidated Freightways (James had renamed the company) and five other western carriers formed the Freightways Manufacturing Company in 1940, to build trucks for their own fleets. The company's first manufacturing plant was opened in Salt Lake City, Utah.

James' lightweight COE design was the first truck to be produced. By this time, it had been improved upon even more – with a heat-treated steel alloy frame and nose for durability. Of course, the aluminium cab and trailer body would be its most distinctive and profitable feature.

But even after opening the Salt Lake City plant, James wasn't really planning to get into the manufacturing business permanently. He just wanted to build enough trucks to supply himself and the other carriers he'd gone into business with. That all changed when the Freightways Manufacturing Company decided to try to outsource the assembly of its trucks. James and his partners were quickly convinced that the products assembled outside their own plant were vastly inferior to those they'd assembled themselves. That was how Freightways stepped into the manufacturing business permanently, and how what was to become the Freightliner brand of truck was eventually born.

## Specifications

**Country:** USA
**Year manufactured from:** 1940s
**Engine:** Cummins diesel powered
**Transmission:** not available
**Payload:** not available
**Applications:** long haul
**Special features:** use of aluminium in parts, bodies and cabs

Below: *James Leyland convinced five other western USA carriers to form the Freightways Manufacturing Company in 1940, to build trucks for their own fleets.*

ALBION
**1940s UK**

# ALBION 6x4 THREE-TON REPAIR TRUCK (MODEL FT103N)

Towards the end of World War II, many British Army trucks were in pretty poor shape. Many of them had been designed before or at the beginning of the war, and had been overhauled several times since.

The army needed a truck on the front line that could repair existing vehicles and carry spares to those who needed them. Because of a dearth of commercially available trucks, they decided to make a limited purchase of Albion 3-ton commercial trucks as a stopgap.

### Off-road use

The Albion trucks purchased had simple commercial chassis, with six wheels and four-wheel drive. They did not have off road suspension, but as far as the British Army was concerned, they fitted the bill.

The repair trucks carried a lathe, pillar drills, bench grinders, gas-welding equipment, battery charges and assorted equipment. The standard Albion Clansman commercial vehicle cabs were used. The bodies had canvas tops and wooden sides, which could be folded down to provide ground-level workbenches. Canvas shelters could even be attached to the sides of the vehicle to provide more workspace on the ground. The FT repair truck was 6.32m (20ft 9in) long, 2.28m (7ft 6in) wide and 3.35m (11ft) high with a 3.58m (11ft 9in) wheelbase.

Right: *The Albion FT103N repair truck was an adaptation of a 6x4 civilian model.*

## Specifications

**Country:** UK
**Year manufactured from:** 1940s
**Engine:** four cylinder diesel
**Transmission:** chain or worm drive
**Payload:** 3.04 tonnes (three tons)
**Applications:** military
**Special features:** sides of bodies could be folded down to provide work benches

PACIFIC CAR AND FOUNDRY

1942 USA

# PACIFIC CAR AND FOUNDRY M26 COE

Today PACCAR is best known for having sold various heavy-duty trucks under various famous brand-names, including Kenworth, Peterbilt, DAF, Leyland and Foden.

## Specifications

**Country:** USA

**Year manufactured from:** 1942

**Engine:** diesel powered

**Transmission:** four-speed forward transmission with three-speed central transfer case

**Payload:** 12.2 tonnes (12 tons)

**Applications:** military tank hauling

**Special features:** three axles

Above: *The Pacific Car and Foundry Company of Renton, Washington were responsible for building the US Army's most powerful tractor, the Pacific M26, used to haul tank transporters.*

Pacific Car and Foundry wouldn't build a truck until 1942, when it was commissioned to do so for wartime use by the American armed forces. The US Army needed a vehicle that would be powerful enough to haul tanks loaded onto semi-trailers. And Pacific Car and Foundry would deliver just that, when the M26 rolled off its production line.

The M26 would be one of the most powerful trucks built during the war. It was a 6x6, in a cab-over-engine truck-tractor design that could pull 12.2 tonnes (12 tons). It had three axles and a Hall-Scott diesel engine that could develop 178.9kw (240hp). It used a four-speed transmission with a three-speed central transfer case that connected to the rear eight-wheel tandem drive as well as the front two-wheel steering axle (by shaft).

### Made for tank and trailer recovery

The truck also had a winch mounted at the front and controlled from the cab and capable of pulling 15,876kg (35,000lb), so it could recover any tractor or trailer lodged in rough terrain. Two more winches were mounted at the rear of the cab.

GMC
1940s USA

# GMC CCKW SERIES AND OTHER WARTIME TRUCKS

The GMC CCKW series of military trucks were made from 1941 to 1945, specifically for the US military during World War II. No fewer than 600,000 Model 353s and 25,000 Model 352s were produced in just four years.

They came in several different shapes and sizes, for example, the CCKW-353 had a 4.1m (13ft 8in) wheelbase and was a 6x6, while the CCKW-352 was a 6x4 with a 3.7m (12ft 1in) wheelbase. Both trucks weighed about 2500kg (5512lb). Both trucks had six-cylinder overhead-valve diesel engines that could develop up to 67.1kw (90hp) and a maximum speed of 72km/h (44.7mph). The 353 and the 352 both had five-speed overdrive-style gearboxes with two-speed transfer cases, and could go about 400km on 182 litres of fuel (about 16 miles per gallon). Both trucks were available with hard or soft cabs, and with or without winches. But America wasn't the only country producing GMC trucks.

## Germany takes over

When World War II began in Europe, Germany nationalized the GMC Opel Division. The plant immediately started producing trucks for the Axis powers. By then GM had been established in Europe for

Above: *If one truck stuck in the minds of World War II veterans it was the ubiquitous 'Jimmy' 2.54-tonne (2.5-ton) 6x6. The GMC CCKW and its 6x4 sister the CCW were built in vast numbers.*

some time. In 1923, GM's first European assembly plant was opened in Copenhagen under the name General Motors International A/S. It was to build Chevrolets for sale in Scandinavian countries, the Baltics, Germany, Poland, Czechoslovakia, Austria, Hungary and Russia. The first GM vehicle to come off the Copenhagen assembly line at the beginning of 1924 was also the first GM to be built outside North America – it was a Chevrolet utility truck. GM went on to establish operations in Antwerp, Belgium, in 1924.

Vauxhall Motors Ltd., Luton, England, was acquired by General Motors in 1925. The same year saw General Motors Export Division open its first warehouse in Malaga, Spain, as well as a sales office in Paris and a warehouse in Le Havre, France. Also in 1925, GM opened a sales office in Berlin.

The year 1927 would also see a GM assembly plant built in Berlin. By 1929, GM had acquired Adam Opel AG, based in Rüsselsheim, Germany. Opel would be taken over by the German government in 1940. One might say GM took the war personally.

## Dedicated to the war effort

The company converted 100 per cent of its production to the war effort as of 1942. During World War II, GM delivered more than $12,300,000,000 worth of war material to lead the Allied war effort, including aircraft engines, aircraft parts, trucks, tanks, marine diesels, guns, shells and miscellaneous products.

In 1942 alone, the company would produce 148,111 power units solely for military use, which amounted to 16.9 per cent of the total truck production in the US that year. By 1943, the company would produce no less than 16 different trucks for the US Army. They included 1½- to 3-ton small-arms repair trucks, 1½-ton radio transceiver trucks, 1½- to 3-ton air-compressor trucks, 2½-ton 6x6 artillery tractors, 2½-ton 3400-litre (750-gallon) tankers, 1½- to 3-ton machine-shop trucks, 2½-ton cargo and troop transporters, 2½-ton cavalry haulers, 1½- to 3-ton earth-boring trucks, 1½-ton recruiting trailer trucks, 2½-ton searchlight carriers, 8-ton arsenal tractor trailers, COE navy fuel tankers, 4-ton anti-aircraft defence trucks, and 1½-ton 4x4 troop transporters.

GMC also produced an estimated 560,000 2½-ton 6x6 trucks for general use. But perhaps the most distinctive vehicle built by GMC during World War II was the amphibious DUKW, know as the 'Duck'. The vehicle looked like a boat with six wheels (duals in back) and a soft-top. It was designed to carry up to 50 men on either land or water.

Inset: *It was basic in design but the famous 'Jimmy' was the mainstay of the Allied Forces in World War II.*

## Specifications

**Country:** USA
**Year manufactured from:** 1941
**Engine:** six cylinder overhead valve diesel and petrol powered
**Transmission:** five-speed overdrive with two-speed transfer case
**Payload:** variable
**Applications:** military
**Special features:** available with hard or soft cabs

Below: *The amphibious variant of the CCKW, designated DUKW, would traverse land and water equally and could cope with 50 fully equipped soldiers. The vehicles were nicknamed 'Ducks'.*

INTERNATIONAL
1947 USA

# INTERNATIONAL KB

In 1947 International continued its K series of trucks with the introduction of the KB. The new KB had a wide grille which extended out on the front wings.

Right: *International's KB series of trucks had a full range of sizes, including this pick-up truck. Despite their small size, they were used for a wide range of hauling tasks. Before long, trucks of a similar design were surfacing in other parts of the world.*

The KB series didn't enjoy a particularly long production span, only being built between 1947 and 1949. During this time, production numbers were quite high, however. For instance about 64,000 KB-5s alone were constructed during this period. This was largely attributable to the post-war demand for trucks.

## Panel bodies

The smaller models had panel bodies and could be used to haul modest loads. Wooden boxes could be found on the back of each of the models allowing for freight haulage. These trucks were commonly equipped with dump bodies. Tractor versions were also available for hauling semi-trailers.

It was a stylish-looking truck with a sleek front-end and large round headlamps. A long conventional-style bonnet provided the truck with a big-truck look and feel. It also carried the relatively new International logo featuring a red 'I' over a black 'H'. Today, the KB series of trucks are popular choices for truck restorers. The largest of the KB series, the KB-8 had an International 5.9-litre (360ci), 93.9kw (126hp) Red Diamond engine under its bonnet.

Typical specs on the KB-1 included a heavy-duty clutch, rear heavy-duty springs, West Coast mirrors and split-rim wheels with eight-ply tyres. The popularity of the KB series of trucks was noticed overseas as well as in North America.

## Specifications

**Country:** USA
**Year manufactured from:** 1947
**Engine:** up to an International 5.9- litre (360ci), 193.9kw (126hp) Red Diamond
**Transmission:** four-speed to bevel
**Payload:** 1.016 tonne (1 ton)
**Applications:** local pick-up and delivery.
**Special features:** this series only enjoyed two years of production, yet was a highly popular truck during that post-war era.

FREIGHTLINER

**1947 USA**

# FREIGHTLINER MODEL 800 'BUBBLENOSE'

Freightliner introduced its all-aluminium 'Bubblenose' Model 800 cab-over-engine in 1947. The company was prospering in the post-war years and it was aggressively pursuing the use of aluminium in its truck parts.

## Specifications

**Country:** USA

**Year manufactured from:** 1947

**Engine:** Cummins diesel

**Transmission:** not available

**Payload:** not available

**Applications:** long-distance, on-highway

**Special features:** one of the first mainstream trucks to fully utilize aluminium in an effort to minimize weight and maximize payloads.

Above: *Freightliner's Bubblenose may have looked a bit unusual, but its aluminium composition allowed carriers to increase payload by about a tonne (0.98 ton).*

Aluminium alloys were being widely used in Freightliner's cabs, axle housings, brake drums, cross members, wheels, radiators and even frame rails. The company was adamant about developing a lightweight vehicle that didn't compromise strength or safety. By doing so, Freightliner trucks were able to haul 1 tonne (0.98 ton) more payload than most other trucks on the market.

The company had plenty of incentive to maximize payload as the first Freightliners were built by and for Consolidated Freightways. Since Freightliner's birth it had been providing Consolidated Freightways with reliable transportation. However, engineers had now built a truck that was deemed ready to compete on the open market. The very first sale came in 1948 to Vince Graziano, a Portland, Oregon-based fruit and vegetable haulier. The Model 800 all-aluminium Bubblenose was the truck that Graziano took delivery of and he was so impressed by the truck that he ordered five more shortly thereafter.

In 1949 Freightliner offered a sleeper-cab version of its trucks. In 1951 the company put White Motor Company in charge of sales, service and distribution of Freightliners.

VOLVO
1953 **Sweden**

# VOLVO VIKING L38

In the early 1950s Volvo unveiled what would become one of its most famous trucks ever – the Viking. It seemed a fitting name for the model since both Volvo itself and the ancient Vikings originated in Scandinavia.

The Viking was based on Volvo's L24 Roundnose truck. When first introduced, the Viking featured only a new bonnet and wings. However, the manufacturer continued to enhance the Viking throughout the 1950s and into the early 1960s. Volvo continuously updated not only the engine strength of the Viking but also its chassis. Power steering was another feature that wasn't available on the earliest models.

## International appeal

The Viking gained worldwide appeal due largely to its reliability, but it was not an overly powerful truck. In the 1950s, enormously powerful engines weren't required for road transport in most of Europe since heavy loads were not yet the norm. The Viking was powered by a modest nominal 7-litre (424.9ci) engine which was known for its dependability, if not its power. The original Viking engine had an output of just 74.5kw (100hp).

Throughout the 1950s, the engine received power upgrades to keep up with trends in the road transport industry. In 1954, a genuine 7-litre (424.9ci) engine was introduced (the initial one was actually just over 6 litres [364.2ci]) along with wider wings resembling the ones that could be found on Volvo's L39 Titan – the Viking's bigger, more powerful cousin.

The majority of Vikings manufactured were two-axle versions, however a three-axle variant was available as well. Production of the Viking ended in 1965 when it was replaced by the similar-looking N86.

Above: *The Viking was one of Volvo's most famous trucks ever.*

## Specifications

**Country:** Sweden
**Year manufactured from:** 1953
**Engine:** Volvo 7 litre (424.9ci) up to 74.5kw (100hp).
**Transmission:** not available
**Payload:** not available
**Applications:** long-distance, on-highway, logging, off-highway
**Special features:** the Viking established itself as one of Volvo's most famous trucks to ever take the highway.

BEDFORD

1950s UK

# BEDFORD

After the war Bedford resumed production of its trucks using the K, M and O models introduced in 1939 as its base. However, it wasn't long before the company replaced those trucks with more current offerings.

Above: *This S type Bedford was dubbed 'The Big Bedford'.*

## Specifications

**Country:** UK
**Year manufactured from:** 1950s
**Engine:** full range of Bedford petrol engines
**Transmission:** four-speed
**Payload:** 7 tonnes (6.8 tons)
**Applications:** long-distance, on-highway, military, local pick-up and delivery.
**Special features:** Bedford produced full range of commercial vehicles following World War II.

The S type was known as 'The Big Bedford' and it vaulted the manufacturer into the 7-tonne (7-ton) class. The truck also featured a new forward-control design. The S type was powered by a 4.9-litre (300ci) petrol engine. It was replaced by the low-cab forward-control TK in 1960. Later is was offered with Leyland and Perkins diesels.

### R type embraced by the military

The four-wheel drive R type derivative was designed in 1950 and quickly embraced by the military, where it served as its standard 4-tonne (3.9 ton) truck until being replaced by the MK and MJ types, and then hit the civilian market in 1953. Meanwhile, Bedford had produced the CA van, which went on to become one of its best-sellers.

In 1953 Bedford continued its aggressive product launch with the introduction of the A type, which was followed by the D and J types. These models were built well into the 1970s, with the exception of the A type which was terminated in 1957.

The J type (or the TJ) was launched in 1958 – the same year Bedford produced its millionth truck. It featured a single-piece windscreen and 40.6cm (16in) road wheels providing a low body platform height on models up to 4 tonnes (3.9 tons). The TJ had a bonneted cab.

PETERBILT
1950 USA

# PETERBILT 280/350

Peterbilt founder T.A. Peterman passed away in 1945 and it was a tragedy that he never lived to see one of the most innovative of the truck company's products – the Model 280/350 'Bubblenose'.

This truck was developed in response to a growing Interstate highway network which was making long-distance freight haulage by truck more practical than ever. Because not all American truckers were fond of the cab-over-engine appearance, the company also released the 281/351 conventional-styled trucks. As a result, Peterbilt had its bases covered when it came to the on-highway market.

## The Bubblenose

Things were looking good for Peterbilt in 1950. The company had reached sales of

Above: *The Pete 350 'Bubblenose' was a cross between a conventional and cab-over design. Most American truckers preferred a conventional truck design, but this style incorporated the best of both worlds.*

$7 million and the trucking industry was becoming increasingly enamoured with the truck. Still, in the rapidly changing transport industry no company could rest on its laurels and it was necessary to continue exploring new technologies and treading new territory. Thus, the 280/350 'Bubblenose' was born.

The 280/350 model was referred to as the 'Bubblenose' because it did not have a flat front like other cab-over-engines. Instead, the engine protruded slightly from the front of the cab, giving the truck what looked like a small, rounded nose. However, that nose was far shorter than the traditional conventional-style bonnets of the day and the truck was classified as a cab-over-engine. Some truckers speculated the Bubblenose resulted from a shortening of the 1949 Model 360, which had a short nose that resembled a half-bonnet conventional.

## COEs gain acceptance

The Bubblenose's cab was perched quite high compared to other models on the road at the time. The engine could be accessed by tilting the cab, but this wasn't easy to accomplish according to some truckers. They often chose to access the engine and other components by swinging the front wings out of the way.

Two years of road testing went into the 280/350 before it was mass-produced for sale to the public. The Bubblenose was a popular truck as it adhered to length restrictions being imposed in some states, especially in the eastern USA.

The Bubblenose was replaced by the 352 in 1955. The 352 was a redesigned cab-over featuring a slightly-curved four-piece windscreen and it remained in Pete's product line until 1982 when the Model 362 superseded it. The 362 would have a more modern one- or two-piece flat windscreen.

## The 281 and 351 conventionals

Introduced in 1954, the 281 and 351 conventional models gave customers an alternative to the Bubblenose. These trucks were well-liked by drivers and owners and remained in production for 11 years. They were among the first to be adorned with Peterbilt's signature red oval logo. Ironically, cab-over-engine versions of these models were introduced in late 1955.

## Specifications

**Country:** USA

**Year manufactured from:** 1950

**Engine:** Cummins or GM

**Transmission:** 10-speed

**Payload:** not available

**Applications:** long-distance, on-highway

**Special features:** these trucks helped pioneer the Drom-Box – cargo boxes attached to the back of the tractor.

Left: *The 351 was the all-American classic 'conventional' tandem drive tractor, seen here with a typical sleeper compartment mounted behind the cab.*

DIAMOND T

1950s USA

# DIAMOND T 950-951

Diamond T had made a name for itself during the war by producing what were widely thought to be the best-looking trucks in which to do battle. However, the post-war years would not be so kind to the company.

One post-war innovation was the development of a 'comfort cab' which was built in conjunction with International Harvester. The 1950 cab featured a number of enhancements such as detachable wings and a bonnet that allowed outside air to pass into the engine compartment to provide better cooling and improved fuel economy. The cab also featured a four-point 'diamond' mounting of the cab, sheet metal and radiator and had a curved windscreen and concave instrument panel.

To prove how well the cab was constructed, the company subjected it to hours of severe twisting at the Chicago Auto Show that year, but no structural damage took place.

## Diamond T 950-951 introduced

That same year, Diamond T introduced its 950 and 951 series of trucks, which were built at the company's Chicago factory. The 950 was built with Western truckers in mind, as they tended to demand more horsepower and larger radiators to provide adequate cooling for the larger engines. The 950 and 951 Diamond Ts were so big that, although they were a conventional design, the driver

Above: *The Diamond T 921-C tilt cab trucks of the mid-1950s could gross up to 34.5 tonnes (38 tons) and had a choice of Cummins diesels.*

was often perched as high as he would be in a cab-over truck.

## Diesel takes over

The first of these trucks to hit the streets were equipped with petrol engines. However, those soon gave way to the more efficient diesel-powered engines. In 1953 these trucks were paired with the tilt-cab.

In the 1950s Diamond T was focusing exclusively on the heavy-duty truck market and was only building trucks with 3 tonnes capacity or greater. The 950 and 951 were the largest offerings and were typically powered by a 223.7kw (300hp) Cummins diesel engine or a 208.7kw (280hp) Buda diesel.

Diamond T also built a handful of 950 RS trucks which may well be the largest Class 8 trucks ever built for on-highway applications. It has been reported that less than 80 of these trucks were ever built. They were powered by Cummins diesel engines.

## Diamond T honoured

In 1953 Diamond T's tilt-cab cab-over-engine truck was presented with the prestigious National Design Award for an industrial project. It was the first time any truck design had won this coveted prize. The technology which earned Diamond T the award was a counterbalance system, which no longer made it necessary for a power unit to tilt the model 723C cab. This development was adopted by other truck makers in years to come.

## The last pre-acquisition Diamond Ts

While the trucking industry was awash with rumours regarding the impending acquisition of Diamond T, the company continued releasing new models. During the 1950s the company built 6x6 trucks for the military which were powered by 167kw (224hp) Continental R6602 engines. The trucks featured automatic six-wheel drive and power steering.

The year before Diamond T was acquired by White Motor Company, it introduced the Model 831 which was driven by a 178.2kw (239hp) Hall-Scott 590 engine. This engine could burn liquid petroleum gas, which boosted its power to 190.8kw (256hp). A tilt-cab model 911C diesel was also offered before Diamond T was taken over.

Diamond T was experiencing trouble by the late 1950s. Its competitor Reo was also struggling to compete with the big players such as International, GM and White. White Motor Company stepped in and purchased both companies in 1958 and consolidated the two brands.

Left: *The tilt-cab design of the Diamond T won it the coveted National Design Award in 1953. It marked the first time a truck design had ever received the award.*

## Specifications

**Country:** USA
**Year manufactured from:** 1950s
**Engine:** 223.7kw (300hp) Cummins diesel engine or a 208.7kw (280hp) Buda diesel
**Transmission:** 10-speed to bevel
**Payload:** not available
**Applications:** long-distance, on-highway, construction, off-highway
**Special features:** Diamond T gained fame during World War II and was known as the 'best looking trucks to do war.'

Below: *The tilt cab fitted to Diamond T medium-weight trucks from the early 1950s had a modern appearance and was imitated by other manufacturers in subsequent years.*

MACK
1953 USA

# MACK G, H AND B SERIES

The 1950s were busy years for Mack, which introduced a number of advancements to its product line. The G, H and B series trucks were among the most significant developments from the company.

In 1953 Mack introduced its new Thermodyne open chamber, direct-injection diesel engine which set a new standard in performance and fuel efficiency. Mack's decision to make its own engines available on its trucks was seen as a bold move at the time. Other engines, including those produced by Cummins, could also be specified.

## H series

The H series was introduced in 1953 and was dubbed the 'Cherry Picker' because of its extremely high cab (2.7m [8ft 10in]). This

Above: *Nicknamed the 'cherry picker', this truck featured an elevated driver's seat. The short BBC measurement allowed it to haul 10.6m- (35ft-) trailers.*

truck had a very short BBC which allowed it to haul 10.6-m (35-ft) trailers. At the time the maximum overall legal length limit in many regions was 13.7m (45ft), making this a practical configuration.

They were typically powered by Mack's ENDT 673 Thermodyne, which produced up to 157.3kw (211hp) at 2100rpm. A Quadruplex 18-speed, two-stick gearbox was another common spec. The Cherry Pickers were replaced by Mack's popular Ultra-Liner.

## B series

The B series, also introduced in 1953, became one of Mack's most successful products to hit the highway. It was an easily identifiable truck due to its stylish, rounded appearance. The cab resembled that of a 1940s-style pick-up truck rather than the big, boxy highway tractor cabs typical of this era.

More than 127,000 of these trucks were sold before production was discontinued in 1966 in favour of the R series. This line of trucks was known for its longevity and many of them are still in active service.

## G series

Mack began production of the G series in 1959 and produced a total of 2181 units by 1962. The truck featured an all-aluminium cab to reduce its weight and to allow for the haulage of heavier loads.

Inset: *The stylish, rounded appearance of Mack's B series made it an instant hit with North American customers. The truck was a refreshing change from the 'boxy' truck designs that dominated the highway at the time.*

Below: *The G series featured an aluminium cab which made it possible to haul heavier loads. It was especially popular in the West Coast region of North America.*

## Specifications

**Country:** USA

**Year manufactured from:** 1953

**Engine:** Thermodyne open chamber, direct-injection diesel or Cummins

**Transmission:** Quadruplex 18-speed, two stick

**Payload:** not available

**Applications:** long-distance, on-highway, severe-service

**Special features:** H series 'cherry picker' provided high sitting position for improved view of the road.

DAIMLER-BENZ

1955 Germany

# DAIMLER-BENZ LP SERIES

Daimler-Benz introduced its LP series of cab-over-engine trucks in 1955 when the LP 315 7-tonne truck took to the roads. The 'P' in this series stood for 'Pullman' in reference to the comfort of a Pullman car's cab.

Above: *The LP series of Mercedes-Benz trucks had a cab that was intended to reflect the interior of a luxury car. To reiterate this point, the 'P' in LP stood for 'Pullman' – a popular luxury car of that era.*

The new trucks lacked the classic wings and cab shape the previous generation of L series trucks were known for, and instead it had a rounded, comfortable cab design with an interior likened to that of a luxury car.

## The dawn of the cab-over-engine

Prior to the introduction of the LP series, most of Daimler-Benz's trucks were bonneted. However COE trucks were beginning to find their place in the market. The LP 315 was joined in 1958 by the LP 333 twin-steer six-wheel truck which had a 16-tonne (15.7-ton) gross vehicle weight or 32-tonne (31.5-tons) gross train weight. It was the first year the German government had given the green light to such heavy loads.

## The LPS333 is added

An LPS333 tractor was also introduced to the market and it was also rated at 32 tonnes (31.5 tons) gross combination weight. This truck's second steering axle was mid-mounted 1.6m (5ft 3in) ahead of the drive axle. Each of the LP trucks featured a full-width cab and a split windscreen. However the LP 321, LP 322 and LP 337 would later be available with a smaller cab and single windscreen. These later additions to the LP family were offered with payloads of 6 to 7 tonnes (5.9 to 6.8 tons).

## Easier to understand design codes

By 1963 Daimler-Benz's cab-over-engines had undergone many changes. The LP 1620 was introduced with a gross weight of 16 tonnes (15.7 tons) and a 149kw (200hp) engine. The model names which were obscure in the 1950s to say the least, were now easier to understand. The LP 1620, for example, referred to its gross weight and the engine horsepower.

Customers were impressed with the cab's simple, cubic design. Extended versions of most models were released with the option of a sleeper compartment for long-distance hauls. The new generation of LP trucks were generally driven by Daimler-Benz's proven six-cylinder in-line engines featuring an efficient direct-injection system and power ratings in the 156.5kw (210hp) range. It wasn't long before three-axle trucks were added to the product line.

## Lightweight LPs

A new lightweight series of LP trucks was also introduced consisting of trucks with weights starting at 6 tonnes (5.9 tons) (LP 608). These cab-over-engines eventually replaced the short-nose trucks Daimler-Benz had been producing. This line of lightweight COEs was designed to look much like its bigger cousins with an angular cab, rectangular grille and attractive glazing. The light LP cabs were firmly mounted to the frame and were not tiltable.

## More powerful engines demanded

In the mid-1960s Daimler-Benz launched the LPS 2020 three-axle rear-steer tractor unit, which was engineered to capitalize on an increase in allowable weights from 32 tonnes to 38 tonnes (31.4 tons to 37.4 tons). Because of the heavier loads anticipated as a result of the regulatory change, more powerful engines were required.

Daimler-Benz developed a new series of engines to meet these new demands and offered them in V6, V8, V10 and V12 sizes. Their power capabilities ranged from 143.1kw to 298.2kw (192hp to 400hp).

Some of the first trucks to be matched with engines from the new family were the LP and LPS 1632, 2032 and 2232 models. These trucks were identifiable because of their deep front wheel arches. The first of the new engines to hit the road was the OM403 which was a 16-litre (976ci) V10.

As a result of all these new vehicle introductions, Daimler-Benz had developed a broader product line than any other commercial manufacturer of the day. The company was a player in nearly all significant sectors of the trucking industry.

## Specifications

**Country:** Germany
**Year manufactured from:** 1955
**Engine:** Daimler-Benz six-cylinder in-line engines
**Transmission:** four-speed to bevel
**Payload:** not available
**Applications:** long-distance, on-highway, local pick-up and delivery.
**Special features:** LP line of trucks catered to virtually every application and GVW range.

Below: *With the German government allowing heavier loads than ever, the LP was put to work delivering a range of heavy freight.*

DAF
1957 **Netherlands**

# DAF 2000 SERIES

DAF decided to plunge into the international transport sector in 1957 with the introduction of its 2000 series. It was a short-lived experiment, however, with the line being discontinued just two years later.

It was a unique truck, with a 10-tonne (9.8-ton) capacity rear axle – the only truck to offer this at the time. The cab was based on the A1300/1600/1800 series cab; however, more room was added at the front to provide more cooling power.

## Normal control vehicle

At about the same time the 2000 series was made available, DAF also released a normal control vehicle for specific market segments. This was known as the 12 and 15 series. In 1958, DAF began the in-house production of axles and this resulted in the need for a completely new factory. The new facility was built at Oevel, near Westerlo in Belgium. It remains in use for the production of axles today.

Above: *The 2000 model of 1957 was DAF's first truck designed for long-distance international haulage. Just five years after its launch it was superseded by the much improved 2600 model.*

## The Eurotrailer unveiled

DAF continued adding new products to complement the 2000 series. One new addition to the product line was the Eurotrailer, introduced in 1962. This was a lightweight semi-trailer with an integral aluminium body. DAF also surprised many during the same year by adding the 2600 truck to its lineup.

The DAF 2600 had a compact design that enabled increased payload and longer load lengths. The truck was able to accommodate a sleeper for long-distance haulage. It was quickly dubbed 'The Mother of International Road Transport'.

## DAF 2600 added

The 2600 launched DAF into the realms of the most respected long-distance truck manufacturers because of its increased driver comfort. It also helped DAF attain increased market share and sales and in 1964 the company produced its 50,000th truck chassis. The following year, DAF founder Hub van Doorne retired after leading his company to success. During his reign, the company had acquired more than 100 patents.

In 1973 DAF replaced the illustrious 2600 with the 2800 which featured a 20cm (7.8in) wider cab. The sleeper cab could fit two full-size beds and the truck was powered by an 11.6 litre (704ci) DAF engine.

## Specifications

**Country:** Netherlands

**Year manufactured from:** 1957

**Engine:** not available

**Transmission:** six-speeds to bevel

**Payload:** not available

**Applications:** long-distance, international, on-highway

**Special features:** this truck was ultimately unable to make an impression in the long-distance international transport segment.

Below: *Day and sleeper versions of the old DAF cab were available. The day cab shown here is on a 4x4 model for on/off-road building work.*

GMC

**1960 USA**

# THE NEW GMCS

In 1960 GMC completely redesigned its popular line of light-duty trucks. While light-duty in size and category, these trucks were routinely put to work hauling freight or working on North American farms.

Above: *The GMC L5000 tilt-cab model had a 180 bhp V6 petrol engine. The heaviest L range models had the option of a GM V-71 two-stroke diesel engine.*

Right: *The newly-designed aluminium tilt-cab cruiser was nicknamed the 'Crackerbox'.*

The new design was radically different than its predecessor in both appearance and functionality. The new-look GMC featured a new front and rear suspension for an improved ride, and also boasted more power. They were equipped with a standard V6 engine as of 1960.

## Heavy-duty cousins

While the American public was raving about the new-look light-duty GMCs, its larger cousins were also being put to work in numerous applications. The L-model was a 1.8m (72in) steel tilt-cab truck powered by a choice of engines ranging from a GMC V6 to a V12. The truck didn't change much from year to year and was discontinued in the late 1970s. The cab-over-engine trucks were commonly customized as fire trucks.

## Crackerbox

At the same time, GMC was also introducing a new aluminium tilt-cab cruiser which was nicknamed the Crackerbox. It was introduced in 1959 and sold until 1968 when it was replaced with the Astro.

The lightweight Crackerbox boasted an extra 827.2kg (1824lbs) of payload compared to other similar trucks and measured only 1.2m (48in) from bumper to the back of cab (BBC). This short BBC also made it ideal for manoeuvring in tight places.

The Crackerbox was renamed the F-model in 1960 and was available with diesel engines or GMC's own petrol-powered engines. The truck was still known for its light weight and high payloads, however, and a sleeper was available. It measured only 56cm (22in) deep behind the driver.

## Specifications

**Country:** USA

**Year manufactured from:** 1960

**Engine:** GMC V6–V12

**Transmission:** 10 speeds to bevel

**Payload:** not available

**Applications:** local pick-up and deliver, long-distance, on-highway, fire

**Special features:** radically new design made these trucks stand out.

KENWORTH

1961 USA

# KENWORTH W900/K100

Two legendary Kenworth trucks were introduced in 1961 – the W900 conventional and the K100 cab-over-engine. The K100 was designed to maximize cargo within state truck-length restrictions.

Above: *Kenworth's W900 (seen here on the left) made famous the long, square bonnet that is still popular today among North American owner-operators.*

## Specifications

**Country:** USA

**Year manufactured from:** 1961

**Engine:** Cummins or Caterpillar six cylinder diesels

**Transmission:** full range

**Payload:** not available

**Applications:** long-distance, on-highway, vocational, off-highway, oilfields

**Special features:** tilt bonnet replaces the previously common butterfly-style bonnet.

The Kenworth W900 featured a classic look that was still popular among North American truckers, with a long bonnet and distinctive cathedral grille.

It found itself being thrust into all sorts of applications from rugged off-highway work to long-distance general freight haulage. The truck could be customized for a variety of tasks, making it a diverse vehicle, and also earned a reputation for being strong and reliable.

The W900 was also designed with driver comfort in mind, which won it fans among the over-the-road crowd. The most common engine on the original W900 was a 223.7kw (300hp) Cummins turbocharged six-cylinder NTC-300. In 1982 a modified W900B was introduced.

The W900 gained plenty of attention when one was called upon to deliver a high-resolution spectrometer magnet which was 36,000 times stronger than the Earth's magnetic field. The load was 42.7m (140ft) long and weighed 107 tonnes (105.3 tons), but this customized W900, with a 335.6kw (450hp) Caterpillar engine and a Spicer 24-speed transmission, was able to transport the unusual shipment from Illinois to Palo Alto, California.

### K100

The K100 was an important addition to Kenworth's fleet as a result of length limitations in eastern states. Operators who insisted on running a long-nose conventional truck in those regions would be forced to sacrifice payload, whereas the shorter K100 allowed fleets to maximize their carrying capacity. Of course the aerodynamics left something to be desired and in 1984 Kenworth introduced the K100E cab-over-engine, which improved air flow.

THAMES TRADER
1962 UK

# THAMES TRADER

The British Ford division launched a new truck in 1958 known as the Ford Thames Trader. With a very unusual bonnet, this truck remained in production until 1965, when it was replaced by the D series.

## Specifications

**Country:** USA
**Year manufactured from:** 1962
**Engine:** full range of Mack diesels
**Transmission:** 10 speeds to bevel
**Payload:** not available
**Applications:** long-distance, on-highway, regional delivery, rubbish
**Special features:** Mack came out with a model for each specific application throughout the 1960s.

The first British Ford truck was sold under the Fordson name. When the production facilities moved from Manchester to the banks of the River Thames, the name 'Fordson Thames' was adopted to give the lorries a distinct identity. The Thames name ran from 1957 to 1965. The Thames Trader was a modern semi-forward-control truck that superseded the ET series. The range catered for loads from 1.52 tonnes (1½ tons) to 7.11 tonnes (7 tons), the latter being the highest payload Ford could offer on a four-wheeler rigid truck. The model number referred to the payload: so the Thames Trader 15 was the light 1½-ton truck, the Model 20 was the 2-tonner, the Model 30 the 3-tonner, the Model 40 the 4-tonner and the bigger Model 70 the 7-tonner. In addition, some short-wheelbase tractors were built for hauling semi-trailers. Two petrol engines, and their diesel derivatives, were offered. The four-cylinder version was a 3.6-litre (220ci) petrol engine, born in 1953 and produced as a diesel variant a year later. This engine was designed for the trucks up to 3.05 tonnes (3 tons). Above this weight, the other engine was a petrol or diesel six-cylinder 5.41-litre (330-cu.in) powerplant. With a total of 121,853 semi-forward trucks built (plus 19,000 normal control cab trucks), the Thames Trader was a great success. Some of them were exported or manufactured in Spain by the Ebro company or produced in Turkey by the Otosan company.

Above: *The Thames Trader was sometimes built as a tractor unit with a small wheelbase (2.74m/9ft), but the rigid trucks were more popular.*

MACK
**1965 USA**

# MACK R SERIES

Mack's R series of vocational trucks introduced in 1965 earned its place in trucking history over the course of nearly four decades. The R series became the world's number one mixer and tipper truck.

Above: *Mack lived up to its tough Bulldog reputation with the legendary R series.*

Right: *The Mack R series is a legendary work truck capable of severe-duty applications. It became a best seller, with more than 360,000 units sold before its 2003 retirement.*

## Specifications

**Country:** USA
**Year manufactured from:** 1965
**Engine:** Mack Maxidyne
**Transmission:** 10 speeds to bevel
**Payload:** not available
**Applications:** mixer, tipper, construction, off-highway
**Special features:** legendary dependability and longevity made this one of the best-selling Class 8 trucks of all time.

The R series itself had big shoes to fill when first introduced as a replacement for the popular B series. However, it was a proven winner, especially when paired with Mack's new Maxidyne constant-horsepower diesel engine and the Maxitorque transmission. The Maxidyne was in fact the first high-torque rise constant-horsepower diesel engine to hit the trucking industry.

The R series trucks were immediately recognizable because of their distinctive square front-end. Some of the R series' selling points were a weight-saving design, bolted construction, a tilt-bonnet and a full range of components for customers to choose from.

The staggering number of R series trucks sold in North America made it the most popular Class 8 vocational vehicle in trucking history. Mack R series customers were fiercely loyal, largely because of the model's dependability and longevity. When the RD was terminated in 2003, it was estimated that more than 200,000 of the R series trucks built over the past 38 years were still in operation.

### RB and DM

While production of the RD was halted in 2003 in favour of the Granite, two other models using the R series cab continued to be built. The RB (axle back) and DM (offset cab) remained in production since the Granite was not yet available in those configurations. However, the majority of R series trucks ceased production in 1989.

PETERBILT
1967 USA

# PETERBILT 359

In 1967 Peterbilt introduced the 359 – a truck that would develop a loyal following of truck enthusiasts and is to this day a fixture at most North American truck shows.

One could argue it was the exterior that won the Pete 359 a devoted following. The truck featured a wide, long bonnet and wide grille that was an instant hit with truckers. It was only available with a tilt bonnet, unlike previous Petes which featured a butterfly-style bonnet that was the bonnet of choice among many drivers. The Peterbilt 359 was a headturner and a big success.

## Rapid expansion

Still, owner/operators who took a great deal of pride in the appearance of their rigs embraced the new truck and by 1969 Peterbilt had to construct a new factory in Madison, Tennessee to keep up with the demand. The company had built 21,000 trucks during the 1960s which was four times the number produced during the previous decade.

## Many engine choices available

Peterbilt offered engines from manufacturers such as Caterpillar, Continental, Cummins and Detroit Diesel. A range of engines, including V6s, V8s, straight-sixes, straight-eights and V12s, were available under the typically large Peterbilt bonnets through the 1960s.

The most common engine spec was the Cummins NH 220 diesel which was typically paired with a Spicer 12-speed transmission. Typical axles during this era at Peterbilt were Timken full-floating hypoid or double reduction and gross vehicle weights were up to 38,095kg (84,000lb). Gross combination weights were a staggering 113,376.6kg (250,000lbs) at the time.

The Peterbilt 359 was incredibly popular until being overshadowed by the 379, which was introduced in 1977.

Above: *The Peterbilt 359 established itself as a favourite among North American owner/operators. Drivers found its long bonnet, wide chrome grille and spacious interior appealing.*

## Specifications

**Country:** USA
**Year manufactured from:** 1967
**Engine:** full range from Caterpillar, Continental, Cummins and Detroit Diesel
**Transmission:** nine, 12 or 15 speeds to bevel
**Payload:** GVWs up to 38,095kg (84,000lb)
**Applications:** long-distance, on-highway
**Special features:** first Peterbilt to feature a tilt bonnet.

FORD
1970 USA

# FORD L AND W SERIES

By 1970 Ford had introduced the new L (or Louisville) range of trucks to replace the normal-control T range. At the same time, Ford brought a new heavy-duty tilt-cab model known as the W series to the market.

Right: *Ford's highly successful Louisville or L-line trucks announced in 1970 carried on in production until the 1990s. They sold well, not only in North America, but in many overseas markets.*

## Specifications

**Country:** USA
**Year manufactured from:** 1970
**Engine:** Cummins, Detroit Diesel, Caterpillar up to 201.3kw (270hp)
**Transmission:** not available
**Payload:** not available
**Applications:** long-distance, on-highway, local pick-up and delivery
**Special features:** these trucks represented Ford's last efforts in the Class 8 market

These trucks were built at what was the world's largest truck factory at the time capable of producing 336 trucks per day!

### Louisville range embraced

The W series trucks featured a 1.32m (52in) BBC and had a square look to the cab. There was also a 2.08m (82in) BBC sleeper-equipped W series truck available. Four different Cummins engines could be matched with these trucks offering a total of 13 different power ratings. Detroit Diesel and Caterpillar engines were also options and most delivered between 186.4 and 201.3kw (250 and 270hp). The L range was extremely successful and was in production for more than 20 years. The L-9000 and LT-9000 in particular were embraced by the trucking industry and many considered these trucks to be the manufacturer's first real successful foray into the conventional diesel haul market.

The W series, on the other hand, received an overhaul in 1975 at which time it was given a new grille that looked much like the one found on the more popular L series. The W series was replaced in the late 1970s by the all-aluminium CL-9000.

In 1997 Ford sold its heavy-duty truck operations to Freightliner.

VOLVO

**1977 Sweden**

# VOLVO F10 AND F12

Volvo made history when it introduced its F10 and F12 trucks in 1977. The Swedish manufacturer revolutionized the trucking industry with these two models, which set a new standard for ergonomics and safety.

Above: *The F12 was capable of extremely demanding duties such as hauling logs through the hilly Scandinavian terrain.*

To help design one of the safest commercial trucks on the road, Volvo established a special group of people who would investigate all truck accidents in Sweden and determine what went wrong. The ultimate goal was to design safer trucks and learn from the mistakes of the past. At the same time, special attention was being given to ergonomics. A more conveniently designed and comfortable truck is ultimately a safer truck. The solutions that were reached by designers and the safety team were not only implemented in the F10 and F12, but in every other Volvo truck developed since then.

Volvo opted to use chassis and driveline components that had been in use since 1973 on the N line of trucks to ensure some commonality between the models. These components had already proven themselves in a wide range of applications and the philosophy of 'If it ain't broke, don't fix it' was followed when it came to these parts.

Instead, Volvo engineers directed their attention to improving safety through other modifications to the vehicle. One new development was fitting the cab to the chassis with a spiral suspension to improve driver comfort and ride. This simple change was able to reduce the back pain suffered by many long-haul truckers.

## Adjustable steering wheel

The steering wheel was made adjustable so the driver could set it at his or her preferred location and angle. In addition, the windscreen size was increased so drivers had better visibility, reducing the risk of an accident. More enhancements for convenience were also introduced into the F10 and F12 models, including a luggage compartment which was accessible from the exterior, but locked from the inside to prevent theft. This was a nice touch for long-distance truckers – the main target market for these trucks.

## Injury prevention a priority

Despite its best efforts, Volvo realized accidents could not be completely eliminated. The company strived to make the interior of the truck as safe as possible so drivers had a better chance of escaping injury in the event of an accident.

Padding was added to the inside of the cab and virtually all sharp edges were eliminated. Naturally the cab was tested to the stringent Swedish cab test standards, which were the most demanding in the world. Driver health was also a motivation for the new integrated air-conditioning system. In Europe, previous air-conditioning systems consisted of air being blown through a single vent, which wasn't healthy for drivers. Volvo's new integrated system alleviated this problem and was another popular feature of the F10 and F12.

## Slightly heavier

Customers were not deterred by the fact that the cab weighed more than some of the other less safety-orientated cabs on the market. For most, the trade-off in weight was worthwhile given the safety enhancements. The F10 and F12 were developed before advanced computer-aided design techniques were available. The F10 and F12 cab featured a flat roof, but the Globetrotter cab was made available in 1979 for operators craving some extra space.

Volvo continuously enhanced the F10 and F12 over the next few years and by the mid-1990s more than 200,000 of these trucks had been sold.

Left: *The F10 and F12 cabs weighed slightly more than other comparable cabs, but customers didn't mind since the safety was enhanced so drastically.*

## Specifications

**Country:** Sweden

**Year manufactured from:** 1977

**Engine:** 9.6-and 12-litre (586 and 732ci) Volvo

**Transmission:** not available

**Payload:** not available

**Applications:** long-distance, on-highway

**Special features:** one of the safest cabs produced at the time.

Left: *Volvo's F10 and F12 trucks set a new standard for safety and ergonomics. The cab was the company's safest yet, thanks in part to the formation of a Volvo Safety Team that investigated accidents and took steps to address any problem areas.*

KENWORTH
1985 USA

# KENWORTH T600A/T800

Kenworth introduced the T600A in 1985, a revolutionary sloped-nose conventional tractor with a set-back front axle. The result was the comfort of a conventional and the manoeuvrability of a cab-over.

At first, truckers were slow to embrace the radical new design. American truckers have traditionally enjoyed the long, square conventional-style bonnets Kenworth and Peterbilt were known for and the new-look T600A took some getting used to. Money talks, however, and with diesel prices reaching new heights it wasn't long before truckers were willing to give it a go.

## Massive fuel savings

The T600A was more aerodynamic than its predecessors, which helped customers shave up to 22 per cent off their fuel costs. Compared with Kenworth's W900 conventional, the T600A delivered 40 per cent less aerodynamic drag. The company admitted it originally feared the radical new styling might turn off some customers. In the end, the gamble paid off as it has earned its spot atop the Kenworth best-seller list.

Still basking in the success of the T600A, Kenworth launched the T800 a year later. This truck featured a set-back front axle for maximum payload and manoeuvrability

Above: *The T600A and the T800 (seen here) accounted for half of Kenworth's production by the mid 1990s.*

but it was designed for heavier-duty operations. It was also suitable for off-highway applications such as logging and mining. The T600 and T800 have been frequently updated since their introduction. The two models accounted for half of Kenworth's production by the mid-1990s. While engineers continue to find ways of saving even more fuel with the T600 and T800 series, unfortunately for truckers the cost of diesel seems to be keeping up with any enhancements.

## Today's T600

Kenworth insists its T600 is without equal when it comes to aerodynamics, performance and driver comfort. It is an ideal truck for linehaul operations (movement of products between two customer locations, for example a local warehouse and a regional distribution centre) due to its exceptional aerodynamics, and its set-back front axle provides excellent manoeuvrability and weight distribution.

The truck can be customized for a range of applications including regional pick-ups and deliveries. Bulk hauliers demanding high payload capacity can also trim it out through a variety of weight-saving options. One could say it's the truck for every job.

Drivers appreciate its quiet cab and conveniently located gauges and controls. It also provides a smooth ride thanks to 162.5cm (64in) front springs, a proprietary eight-bag air suspension as well as a cab/sleeper suspension. Add to all this the fact that the T600 is known for its ease of maintenance and high resale values and it's little wonder the model has proved to be one of Kenworth's successful trucks of all time.

Today's T600 can be matched with a wide range of engines between 10 and 16 litres (610 and 976ci) and up to 447.4kw (600hp). The front axles are available in ratings between 5,454 and 6,636kg (12,000 and 14,600lb) while the rear axles are rated at 10,455kg (23,000lb) for singles and 20,909kg (46,000lb) for tandems. The sleepers that are available on the T600 line from the 96.5cm (38in) AeroCab FlatTop to the more spacious 2.18m (86in) Studio AeroCab.

Left: *The T600A was an immediate hit with long-distance hauliers where fuel mileage was a major concern. The sloped nose remains popular today.*

## Specifications

Country: USA

**Year manufactured from:** 1985

**Engine:** full range up to 447.4kw (600hp)

**Transmission:** nine- or 15-speed to bevel

**Payload:** not available

**Applications:** long-distance, on-highway

**Special features:** sloped bonnet claimed to reduce fuel consumption by 22 per cent.

Below: *The aerodynamic T600A was a radical departure from Kenworth's traditional long-nose conventional-styled truck. While it took some getting used to, even Kenworth loyalists couldn't argue with a 22 per cent fuel savings.*

IVECO

🛠 **1984 Italy**

# IVECO TURBOSTAR

Iveco was founded in the mid-1970s, but it struggled to produce trucks that reflected its own corporate identity. This could be partly attributed to the fact that it was comprised of various factories and companies.

## Specifications

**Country:** Italy

**Year manufactured from:** 1984

**Engine:** Iveco 8210 13.8-litre (842ci), 246kw (330hp), or the Iveco 8280 17.2-litre (1049ci) with 313.1kw (420hp)

**Transmission:** eight-speed to bevel

**Payload:** not available

**Applications:** heavy-duty, long-distance

**Special features:** TurboStar was Iveco's first success in heavy-duty truck market.

Above: *The Turbostar was Iveco's first real success in the heavy-duty long-distance trucking sector. An interior height of 1.7 metres (5ft 6in) made it an ideal truck for long-distance haulage.*

However, in 1984 Iveco introduced the TurboStar, which turned some heads in the trucking industry and helped establish the company as a real player in the commercial vehicle industry. The TurboStar was a huge success in the heavy-duty truck sector. The truck's popularity could be attributed in large part to the cab and engine.

The cab looked similar to those produced by FIAT, but it included many enhancements including an interior height of 1.7m (5ft 7in). The cab was more comfortable than other common cabs of the day and a softer suspension system also contributed to the TurboStar's popularity as it delivered a smoother ride. Iveco referred to the truck as the first real blend of different cultures that had been the focus of Iveco's efforts right from the start. The Iveco TurboStar became famous as the car-haulier of choice for the Ferrari Formula 1 team.

## Most powerful engine available

The TurboStar could be purchased with one of two engines. They included the 8210 13.8-litre (842ci) straight-six turbo with 246kw (330hp), or the 8280 17.2-litre (1049ci) behemoth with 313.1kw (420hp). The latter, a V8, was one of the most powerful engines available in any truck at the time making the TurboStar an ideal truck for heavy-duty haulage. It was particularly popular for long-distance and international transport.

SCANIA 3-SERIES

1988 Sweden

# SCANIA 3-SERIES

Above: *Whilst the Scania 3-series closely resembled its 2-series predecessor, it incorporated numerous refinements to improve performance and reduce emissions.*

Scania introduced its 3-series in 1988 as a successor to the popular 2-series of heavy-duty trucks. Most of the developments incorporated into the 3-series revolved around the powertrain.

Right: *Scania's 3-series was highly customizable and available in a wide range of configurations.*

## Specifications

**Country:** Sweden
**Year manufactured from:** 1988
**Engine:** full range
**Transmission:** five or 10-speed to bevel
**Payload:** not available
**Applications:** long-distance, on-highway
**Special features:** winner of the European Truck of the Year award in 1989.

However, improvements were by no means limited just to the drivetrain components. The 2-series' fascia was replaced with a new, more ergonomic type that curved towards the driver providing easy access to important gauges and instruments. The driver also enjoyed a smoother ride thanks to a cab with four-point suspension.

The Scania 3-series was very well-received by the trucking industry and it took top honours as Truck of the Year in Europe in 1989. It was the first time an entire truck range had won the award. The Truck of the Year jury commented that the 3-series boasted: 'A generally high standard of engineering, top-class driving comfort combined with a high standard of driver and passenger safety, advanced engines offering good fuel consumption and superb reliability.'

### Modular design

With the development of the 3-series, Scania was forging ahead with its modular approach. The manufacturer was producing 'made-to-measure' trucks for specific customers, depending on their individual needs. Customers were able to specify exactly which components they wanted on their vehicle

MACK
1988 USA

# MACK CH

Mack Trucks introduced its CH highway lineup to the North American trucking industry in 1988. The CH was an axle-forward vehicle suitable for on- and off-highway stop-and-go applications.

Left: *Mack referred to its CH series as one of the most versatile trucks on the road. It was put to the test in many applications both on- and off-highway.*

A CH day cab was included in the line, which was ideal for lightweight bulk haul, van, flatbed and lowboy applications, the company said. At the time of its release, Mack said the CH was one of the most versatile trucks on the road, as it could be customized for a wide variety of heavy-duty highway and vocational applications. A range of horsepower ratings were available, which could be paired with various transmissions to deliver optimum performance.

When designing the CH cab, engineers set out to combine the best ergonomic styling with traditional heavy-truck features. For instance, switches and gauges were placed within easy reach of the driver while the fascia was well-lit, making it more visible. The cab was mounted on an air-ride suspension for a smooth ride and view was enhanced as a result of the sloped bonnet.

## Three sleepers

Mack provided three types of sleeper box for the CH series including 1.21m, 1.42m and 1.77m (48in, 56in and 70in) options. Engineers utilized every inch of the cab's space by providing plenty of storage in areas such as the space under the bunk. Improved insulation within the sleeper box provided a more comfortable environment.

## Specifications

**Country:** USA
**Year manufactured from:** 1988
**Engine:** Mack ASET
**Transmission:** 10-speed to bevel
**Payload:** not available
**Applications:** heavy-duty on- and off-highway, vocational
**Special features:** set-forward axle provides excellent manoeuvrability.

KENWORTH
1989 USA

# KENWORTH W 900L

At the end of 1989, Kenworth launched the W 900L (L for 'Long'), with an extended bonnet. It was a special variant of the great W 900, which is still manufactured after more than four decades.

Right: *The Kenworth W 900L remains by far the most stylish American truck in the world, with a massive square radiator and an external stainless air filter.*

## Specifications

**Country:** USA
**Year manufactured from:** 1989
**Engine:** Caterpillar or Cummins up to 447kw (600hp)
**Transmission:** nine- or 15-speed to bevel
**Payload:** up to 200,000 GCW, normally 80,000 GCW
**Applications:** long-distance, on-highway
**Special features:** extended bonnet 330cm (130 inch) BBC, engines up to 447kw (600 hp).

With the introduction of new big six-inline turbocharged and aftercooled engines from Cummins and Caterpillar (up to 447kw/600hp), Kenworth had to change some details of the famous W 900: an extended bonnet and bigger radiator were necessary. The result was the new W 900L. The tilted fibreglass bonnet was so long that it was gently sloped to improve the visibility.

### Classic styling

Of course, the W 900L kept the classic styling of its predecessors, with plenty of chrome, decorative stainless-steel parts and custom upholsteries. There are now 19 interior colour options and three main trim levels (Splendor, Diamond and Diamond VIT – Very Important Truck). For comfort, the handcrafted Studio Sleeper and the Aerocab/Aerodyne Sleepers give the riders plenty of room and a much more homely feel. In order to save weight, the sleepers and the cab are made of corrosion-proof aluminium and fibreglass materials. A modern air suspension system provides a great smooth ride.

With a 330cm (130in) bumper-to-back-of-cabin (BBC) length, the W 900L is specially designed for long-haul applications and hill climbing and for owner/operators. It has a high resale value, and the W 900L remains the spearhead of Kenworth, even if it's not the best seller of the company since the introduction of the T 600 and the T 800.

VOLVO

1993 **Sweden**

# VOLVO FH SERIES

Volvo's FH series, introduced in 1993, has been a true success story for the Swedish manufacturer. The FH12 and FH16 have been heralded as among the most popular trucks ever to take to the highway.

One of the factors contributing to the FH series' success was its cutting-edge technology which helped improve areas such as fuel efficiency. The FH12 was powered by an all-new 12-litre (732ci) D12A engine engineered by Volvo. The FH16, meanwhile, featured a revamped Volvo 16-litre (976ci) engine that was first introduced in 1987 under the bonnet of the F16.

The D12A was designed for use on both sides of the Atlantic. It was the first European-designed diesel truck engine to boast a high-pressure unit fuel injector and overhead camshaft along with four valves per cylinder. This combination provided better breathing for the engine which led to higher efficiency and lower fuel consumption. This technology was previously only found in advanced passenger car engines. It also helped reduce emissions, which was becoming more of an issue in the 1990s.

The D12A also featured Volvo's own engine brake which contributed to the safety

Above: *The FH16 looked much like its less powerful cousin, the FH12, but a 16-litre (976ci) engine provided considerably more power.*

of the new engine. The Volvo Engine Brake was necessitated by the engine's ability to maintain higher average speeds which caused more strain on the brakes. Volvo's Accident Commission – a team that has investigated accidents for more than 25 years – also lent its expertise to the designers to ensure the FH series was as safe as it could possibly be.

## Aerodynamic cab

The FH12 and FH16 featured cabs that were designed with the driver in mind. Fuel efficiency was also a motivation for engineers who designed the cab to be aerodynamic and lightweight without sacrificing any of the creature comforts drivers expected and enjoyed. In fact, while making the cab more efficient and productive, designers also made it quieter and more comfortable. Three cab versions were introduced for the FH12 and FH16. They included a short day cab, long sleeper cab, and long sleeper cab with interior standing room – the Globetrotter. Two years later the even larger Globetrotter XL was introduced.

## More enhancements introduced

The FH became the first heavy-duty truck to be equipped with a driver's side airbag in 1995, according to Volvo. This introduction elevated the truck's passive safety to a whole new level.

In 1998 the FH vehicles received a facelift and the result was the second Truck of the Year Award for the lineup, which was presented in 2000. The FH series received its first such accolade in 1994 following its introduction. The look of the truck changed somewhat as a result of the enhancements. The front of the cab was altered to improve airflow and increase the efficiency of the headlamps. Another safety feature was introduced along with the new FH series at this time – Volvo's new electronically controlled heavy-duty disc brakes.

Another enhancement introduced in the late 1990s was the new D12C engine. It had been completely retooled to provide better performance and greater fuel economy as well as extended service life and even better environmental characteristics. The new engine was developed with impending Euro 3 emissions standards in mind, which were to come into play in 2001.

Volvo halted production of the FH16 in 2001, but in 2003 it came out with a completely new 16-litre (976ci) in-line six cylinder direct-injection diesel engine with overhead camshaft, four valves per cylinder and electronic unit fuel injectors.

Left: *Many truck enthusiasts insist Volvo's FH12 was the most successful truck to ever be built. The critics agreed, naming the FH-series Volvo the Truck of the Year in 1994 and 2000, the first time a single truck won the award twice.*

## Specifications

**Country:** Sweden
**Year manufactured from:** 1993
**Engine:** Volvo D12 A or D16A
**Transmission:** nine- or 14-speed to bevel
**Payload:** 10 to 40 tonnes (9.8 to 39.4 tons)
**Applications:** long-distance, on-highway, logging
**Special features:** Volvo Engine Brake provided stopping power to reduce strain on foundation brakes.

Left: *The FH12 could be purchased with the Globetrotter cab – an enormous cab that allowed a driver to stand up inside. An even larger Globetrotter XL cab was introduced soon after.*

MERCEDES-BENZ
**1996 Germany**

# MERCEDES-BENZ ACTROS

As the successor to the popular 23-year-old Mercedes-Benz SK, the new Actros had big shoes to fill. However, the Actros' engineers strived to deliver improved driver comfort and better performance.

Above: *The Actros cab was designed to stringent safety standards and could be ordered with a driver's side airbag.*

Above, left: *The Mercedes-Benz Actros incorporated new technology such as an automated gearbox that calculated the appropriate gear based on torque and engine speed. It was a popular long-distance highway truck that was easy to drive.*

## Specifications

**Country:** Germany
**Year manufactured from:** 1996
**Engine:** V6 or V8
**Transmission:** MB Telligent gearbox
**Payload:** 24.6 to 27.5 tons (25 to 28 tonnes)
**Applications:** long-distance on-highway
**Special features:** stability control system helps prevent rollovers.

One of the most interesting developments to be implemented in the Actros was the Telligent engine system which was constantly provided with key information so it could make the proper injection duration and timing decisions for each cylinder. The result of this precise engine control was high power output, low fuel consumption and lower emissions.

The Actros also featured a Telligent gearshift system mounted on the side of the seat which could simply be moved up or down to change gears. The Telligent gearbox is able to calculate the appropriate gear and automatically chooses the right one based on torque and engine speed.

The driver could override the gearbox's decision, but in most cases the driver would simply depress the clutch to accept the decision and the truck would change gears accordingly. A rocker switch allows the driver to shift up or down half a gear and if the driver tries to shift into the incorrect gear the system will give a warning.

### Safety first

The Actros' cab was tested to ECE R 29 standards and a driver's side airbag was optional. The optional Telligent roll control system automatically adjusted the shock absorbers based on operating conditions and load characteristics.

KENWORTH
⚒ -996 USA

# KENWORTH T2000

Above: *Twenty years of aerodynamic retooling went into the design of the T2000. Lightweight components were also used to further improve the trucks' fuel mileage.*

Kenworth, traditionally known for its conventional styling, released its aerodynamic highway tractor, the T2000, in 1996. The T2000 was designed to strike a fine balance in pleasing both driver and owner.

## Specifications

**Country:** USA
**Year manufactured from:** 1996
**Engine:** full range 10 to 16 litre (607 to 976ci), up to 447.4kw (600hp)
**Transmission:** nine or 15-speeds to bevel
**Payload:** approx 20.3 tonnes (20 tons)
**Applications:** long-distance on-highway, regional hauling
**Special features:** sloping bonnet provides improved aerodynamics, radically new look.

Above, right: *The T2000 featured a huge, 1.9m (75in) sleeper making it an instant hit with long-distance truckers in the North American market. While it was a departure from Kenworth's long, square bonnet, its improved fuel mileage won it fans among both fleets and owner/operators.*

The truck was unveiled at the International Trucking Show where it was presented in 2.84 and 3.04m (112 and 120in) BBC configurations with 1.9m (75in) AERODYNE sleepers. The cab was bonded and fastened using aerospace technologies that provided a smooth, durable and weather-tight design.

### Twenty years of aerodynamic research

The company said the T2000 was the culmination of 20 years of aerodynamic tooling by the company's engineers. Advanced composite materials, lightweight components and improved aerodynamics combined to make the T2000 a more efficient vehicle to operate in over-the-road applications.

The bonnet, windscreen, fairing, bumper, wings and cab extension were all designed with aerodynamics in mind. Load capacity was also increased thanks to the lightweight components. While setting a new standard for aerodynamics, Kenworth also said the T2000 raised the bar in terms of comfort, performance and reliability and was designed with reducing life-cycle costs in mind.

Drivers were pleased with the T2000's intelligent use of space and ergonomic cab design which contributed to a better lifestyle while on the road. A thermal core floor provided excellent insulating qualities.

DAF
1997 **Holland**

# DAF 95XF

DAF introduced the new 95XF in 1997, promising to deliver lower operating costs, improved reliability and enhanced driver comfort. The truck was named the International Truck of the Year in 1998.

Below: *DAF vowed the 95XF was the perfect truck for heavy and long-distance hauling. The truck's engines boasted up to 396.2kw (530hp) ensuring it could live up to its reputation as a heavy hauler.*

Left: *The DAF XF's Space and Super Space cabs provided plenty of living space for long-haul drivers. More than one cubic metre (35 cubic ft) of storage space was provided with no nook or cranny going to waste.*

The 95-series had been around for 10 years prior to the release of the 95XF. However, the 95XF took the series to a new level, especially in terms of driver comfort.

## Spacious cabs available

Several previously available cab sizes were dismissed on the 95XF in favour of the larger Space and Super Space Cabs. Customers wanting the smaller cab sizes could opt for DAF's more modest 85-series vehicles. Both the Space Cab and Super Space Cab proved to be winners. They not only provided plenty of space, but were also very quiet.

Other features of the Space Cab and Super Space Cab included spacious lockers over the windscreen, a central compartment which could accommodate a microwave oven, and storage underneath the lower bunk. There was also an airtight storage area accessible only from outside the vehicle which could be used to store dirty or smelly objects. The total storage capacity of the Super Space Cab was more than 1 cubic metre (35 cubic feet).

The 95XF provided operators with more powerful engine choices, including Euro-2 and Euro-3 engines ranging from 283.3 to 357.9kw (380 to 480hp). Despite the powerful engines and large cab, the 95XF delivered very good fuel mileage.

## Specifications

**Country:** Netherlands
**Year manufactured from:** 1997
**Engine:** DAF or Cummins up to 395.2kw (530hp)
**Transmission:** 16-speeds to bevel
**Payload:** 25 to 70 tonnes (24.6 to 68.9 tons)
**Applications:** heavy and long-distance hauling
**Special features:** large cabs make it ideal truck for long-distance transport.

SCANIA
1998 Sweden

# SCANIA 4-SERIES

In 1998 Scania released its 4-series of trucks covering the full range of heavy transport requirements from local delivery to long-distance heavy haulage. The 4-series also complied with tough environmental standards.

Above, top: *Driver comfort was one of the top selling points for Scania.*

Above: *The Scania 4-series was environmentally friendly.*

## Specifications

**Country:** Sweden
**Year manufactured from:** 1998
**Engine:** Scania up to 395.2kw (530hp)
**Transmission:** not available
**Payload:** GVW up to 150 tonnes (147.6 tons)
**Applications:** long- and short-distance on- and off-highway, building
**Special features:** compliant with new environmental regulations.

The 4-series was divided into four different classes making it easy for customers to choose the vehicle that best suited their individual needs. Each of the classes boasted a high level of driver comfort and safety and was easy to modify.

The Class L chassis was designed for long-distance haulage on regular roads. This particular truck could handle payloads with gross weights up to of 60 tonnes (59 tons). It could be equipped with engines of up to 395.2kw (530hp). The Class L chassis could be fitted with low, high, high-roof or bonneted day cabs or sleeper cabs. It was the ideal truck for international road haulage.

The Class D chassis featured low maintenance costs and good fuel mileage. The powertrain, chassis and cab were reinforced, providing excellent reliability. It was best suited for short distances on normal roads and had a maximum gross weight of up to 44 tonnes (43.3 tons). Engines of up to 287kw (385hp) could be specified and low day cabs or sleeper cabs were both options.

### A model for every road type

The C class was designed for demanding jobs over short distances, and was an excellent off-road vehicle due to its high ground clearance. The C class could handle gross weights of up to 150 tonnes (147.6 tons) and could be powered by engines up to 395.2kw (530hp). Often, the C class was put to work in the building of heavy special transport sectors. Since the powertrain, chassis and cab were sturdy, this vehicle was very reliable.

FREIGHTLINER
1998 USA

# FREIGHTLINER CENTURY CLASS S/T/ARGOSY

With the turn of the century fast approaching, Freightliner introduced its Century Class S/T in 1998. The new model featured a state-of-the-art aerodynamic design and an under-the-bonnet air-management system.

## Specifications

Class S/T/Argosy
**Country:** USA
**Year manufactured from:** 1998
**Engine:** full range, Detroit Diesel, Mercedes-Benz and Caterpillar
**Transmission:** nine, 12 or 15-speeds to bevel
**Payload:** approx 20 tonnes (19.7 tons)
**Applications:** long-haul, on-highway
**Special features:** COE Argosy able to haul 17.6m (58ft) trailers, increasing load capacity

Above: *With very few cab-over-engine trucks running American highways, Freightliner gambled with the introduction of the Argosy. It allowed operators to haul longer loads, but conventional-style trucks would remain dominant in North America.*

The Mercedes-Benz wind tunnel in Stuttgart, Germany, helped engineers reach new heights when it came to aerodynamics and fuel efficiency, and designers on both sides of the Atlantic contributed to the new model. Safety enhancements such as the introduction of driver's side air bags to the heavy-duty truck market were also achieved.

### Aerodynamic bonnet

The Century Class featured a low, aerodynamic bonnet which provided improved visibility and better fuel consumption as a result of improved air flow over the front of the truck. It was a lightweight, yet strong bonnet constructed of a sheet-moulded compound. A larger windscreen and mirrors also contributed to improved visibility from the driver's seat.

One of the more cutting-edge developments found inside the cab was a Driver Message Center which provided information to the driver such as fuel economy, mileage, fluid levels and other onboard systems. It also provided timely information about any attention or repairs the truck required.

MACK
**1999 USA**

# MACK VISION

Mack introduced its premium highway tractor – the Vision – in 1999. It was designed to provide excellent handling and driver comfort as well as low operating costs and excellent efficiency.

Above: *The Mack Vision was a premium highway tractor with excellent aerodynamics.*

## Specifications

**Country:** USA
**Year manufactured from:** 1999
**Engine:** Mack ASET
**Transmission:** 12 or 16-speed to bevel
**Payload:** 20 tonnes (19.7 tons)
**Applications:** long-haul, on-highway, heavy bulk, tipper
**Special features:** latest generation of engines feature EGR to reduce emissions (as of 2002).

The Vision featured an aerodynamically designed bonnet, grille and cab, giving it a modern highway-tractor appearance. Drivers enjoyed the ergonomic layout of the cab which included an electronic wraparound fascia.

The Vision also provided a smooth ride thanks to the air-suspended cab and sleeper combination. The sleepers were available in a range of sizes including 1.2m (48in) flattop, 1.4m (56in) flattop, 1.5m (60in) mid-rise and 1.7m (70in) mid-rise. The Vision was also available as a day cab for those operators who wanted a lightweight vehicle and didn't require the extra living space afforded by a sleeper cab.

### Vision day cab

The Vision day cab featured an axle-back chassis and could be customized with a variety of axles, transmissions and suspensions. One such suspension was the MaxAir, with 5442.1kg (12,000lb) front and 18,140.5kg (40,000lb) rear axles. For operators planning on putting their Vision to work in flatbed, tipper trailer and heavy-bulk applications, two frames were available including inside channel reinforcement.

MAN
2000 Germany

# MAN TG-A

MAN introduced its Trucknology Generation A as a versatile range built in a modular fashion, which the company said would set the standards for optimum payload. The MAN TG-A won Truck of the Year in 2001.

The 'Trucknology' phrase was coined by MAN executives to describe the advanced engineering and design that went into the TG-A. The truck was launched amid much fanfare in 2000 to an audience of more than 8000 guests at simultaneous events across the United Kingdom.

Modification of the TG-A was still possible thanks to an assortment of wheelbase and overhang combinations available from MAN. Custom bodies could be easily modified to the requirements of a specific job.

## Heavy payloads

The product range included a 6x2 chassis which was capable of taking on jobs involving extremely heavy loads, and five different cabs were available so customers could choose the configuration best suited to their application and haulage distances. MAN referred to this option as a 'space travel' programme for both payload and driver. The MAN TG-A boasted a custom-fit drivetrain and a choice of four Euro 3 compliant engines. Six-cylinder powerplants were the norm, capable of up to 343kw (460hp) while yielding high torque outputs. Despite the power of these engines, they ran quite quietly.

A strong, yet weight-optimized frame helped improve payload capacity on the TG-A. Drivers enjoyed a pneumatic spring system provided enhanced driving stability and a comfortable ride.

Above: *The MAN TG-A trucks, such as these 410 models were known for their high payloads.*

## Specifications

**Country:** Germany
**Year manufactured from:** 2000
**Engine:** MAN 12 and 12.8 litre (732 and 781ci) engines
**Transmission:** 16 or 12-speeds to bevel
**Payload:** 10 to 28 tonnes (9.85 to 27.5 tons)
**Applications:** long-haul, on-highway
**Special features:** optional aerodynamics package reduces fuel usage.

IVECO
2002 Italy

# IVECO STRALIS RANGE

In January 2002, Iveco introduced its Stralis Range line of heavy-duty trucks: first the Active Space model, followed shortly thereafter by the introduction of the Active Time and Active Day models.

Above: *The Iveco Stralis range included the 350 (left) and the 430 (right) heavy-duty models.*

## Specifications

**Country:** Italy
**Year manufactured from:** 2002
**Engine:** Iveco Cursor
**Transmission:** automated EuroTronic 12-speeds to bevel
**Payload:** 28 tonnes (27.6 tons)
**Applications:** local delivery to long-distance international haulage
**Special features:** winner of the 2003 International Truck of the Year award

The Active Space was designed with the long-distance and international haulier in mind. It has plenty of cab room and a large, comfortable sleeper compartment, while the Active Time has been marketed to drivers who haul short or medium distances and don't require a large sleeper box. It does, however, include a bunk and is ideal for short trips of one or two days away from home. The Active Day model is intended for regional delivery drivers who don't sleep in their truck.

### 2003 International Truck of the Year

The Active Space took top honours as the International Truck of the Year in 2003. The cabs of both the Active Time and Active Day were lowered 15cm (5.9in) to make it easier for drivers to enter and exit, reducing driver fatigue. The cab suspension was also modified to reduce vibration.

The major selling point for the Stralis line was its fuel consumption. Company officials boldly claimed the Active Space delivered 4 to 5 per cent better fuel mileage than the competition. This was largely due to a new aerodynamic profile. Each of the Stralis Range models was also designed to reduce maintenance costs. This was achieved through the use of new engine technology.

INTERNATIONAL
**2004 USA**

# INTERNATIONAL 9000I-SERIES

The International 9000i series of highway tractors consists of popular fleet trucks such as the aerodynamic 9200i as well as more conventional-styled trucks such as the International Eagle 9900ix.

## Specifications

**Country:** USA
**Year manufactured from:** 2004
**Engine:** wide range of Caterpillar and Cummins engines
**Transmission:** full range of Fuller and Meritor transmissions
**Payload:** approx 20.3 tonnes (20 tons) on line haul
**Applications:** long-distance transport
**Special features:** aerodynamics make it two-five per cent more fuel efficient than previous models

Above: *The International Eagle became a popular long-distance truck among North American fleets. It features a lightweight, aluminium cab and an aerodynamic bonnet.*

The International 9200i features an aerodynamic shape that makes it between 2 and 5 per cent more fuel efficient than traditional models. It has a set-back front axle to provide improved manoeuvrability and also offers drivers an excellent view of the highway. The truck is lightweight thanks in part to an aluminium cab – another reason for its popularity with fleets which can take advantage of this by hauling longer trailers and heavier loads. The 9200i is also popular with drivers as it boasts an abundance of storage space and plenty of room to move.

### Traditional look

What separates the International Eagle 9900ix is the Eagle trim which can be found inside and outside the cab. The Eagle 9900ix has plenty of stainless steel on the exterior, giving it a classic look as well as a full-width Texas Style front bumper.

RENAULT

2004 France

# RENAULT MAGNUM

Renault's flagship vehicle is the popular Magnum, which can be an effective highway truck operating in most applications. The Magnum is a common sight on European highways.

Above: *The Magnum is Renault's flagship model in Europe.*

Above, top: *The instantly recognizable Diamond badge has been Renault's symbol since 1925.*

## Specifications

**Country:** France

**Year manufactured from:** 2004

**Engine:** E-Tech six cylinder engine

**Transmission:** not available

**Payload:** 2.7 tonnes (2.7 tons)

**Applications:** suitable for all highway applications

**Special features:** Multipass cab delivers 'a true living space'.

What makes the Magnum stand out from other highway trucks is the fact that the cab is physically removed from the driveline components. The Multipass cab sits above, and slightly separated from what the company refers to as the 'technical module' which houses the engine, transmission and other components. The result is a distinctive style and shape that make the Magnum immediately recognizable.

Other unique styling elements incorporated in the latest generation of the Magnum include a flexible spoiler with built-in foglamps and trapezoid, single-piece headlamps that provide excellent visibility at night.

### 'A true living space'

The French manufacturer refers to the Multipass cab as a 'true living space' that provides drivers with an ergonomic driving position, thermal and sound insulation against outside temperatures and noise, as well as reduced warm-up time for added driver comfort. The Multipass cab is designed to reflect an actual apartment, with several distinct areas including a dining room, lounge and bedroom. A swivelling passenger seat represents an armchair, complete with footrest. The latest Magnum also includes plenty of storage space so operators can enjoy more room to move within the cab. The Magnum is a popular choice among drivers because of its many creature comforts.

## Picture Credits

All pictures supplied by Francis Dreer/Big Block except for the following:

3: Scania;
6(t): Volvo;
6(b): Sterling;
7(t): Mary Evans Picture Library;
7(b): Volvo;
8(b): Mary Evans Picture Library;
9: TRH;
11: Daimler-Chrysler;
12: Mary Evans Picture Library;
14-15: Stilltime/Photoshot;
18: Renault;
19: Rex W. Schrader (imaginaryimages.com);
20(b): Renault;
23: TRH;
24: Peter Davies;
25: TRH;
34-35: Peter Davies;
36: Rob English;
38: Volvo;
45(t): Dave Gothard (davesimages.net);
45(b): Peter Davies; .
49: Detroit Public Library;
57: Peter Davies;
64-65: Daimler-Chrysler;
66: DAF;
68(b): Peter Davies;
74(b): Volvo;
75: Volvo;
76(b): DAF;
81: DAF;
84(both): Daimler-Chrysler;
86(both): DAF;
87(both): Scania;
88: Freightliner;
91: Iveco;
93(both): Renault

## Index

skog
SCANIA
460
144G
BFR 543